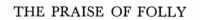

THE PRAISE OF FOLLY

THE PRAISE OF FOLLY

BY DESIDERIUS ERASMUS

Translated from the Latin, with an Essay

& Commentary, by Hoyt Hopewell Hudson

Published by Princeton University Press

at Princeton, New Jersey

Acknowledgments

O F THE THREE ENGLISH TRANSLATIONS OF THE *Praise of Folly* available to me, I have made most use of that by John Wilson, first published in 1668 and reprinted in 1913 by the Oxford University Press, with alterations and an Introduction by Mrs. P. S. Allen. The translation by Sir Thomas Chaloner (1549) is a pleasure to read, but only if one appreciates pre-Elizabethan language and is not discouraged by rather inchoate sentences. The version by White Kennett (1683), which has been often reprinted, usually without the translator's name, is quite untrustworthy, though it corrects Wilson in a few places and displays a highly readable style. A kind of debt I may owe to Kennett—and if a debt at all, then a great one; for it was the badness of his translation which impelled me to undertake my own. The version by James Copner (1878) I have not seen. F. M. Nichols translated the prefatory letter to More and a part of Section 33 in *The Epistles of Erasmus* (1904), Vol. II. I have made some use of the French rendering by J. Nisard, as published in 1842. For the Latin text I have trusted (with two or three slight exceptions) the Le Clerc edition of Erasmus, *Opera Omnia,* Vol. VI (Leyden, 1703).

My introductory essay owes something to Mrs. Allen and more to Dr. Craig Thompson of Cornell University, whose Princeton University doctoral dissertation, *Lucian in the English Renaissance,* underlies my discussion of the

ACKNOWLEDGMENTS

Lucianic elements in this book. Dr. Thompson is preparing a new edition of Bailey's version of the *Colloquies*, a work which will please everyone who reads Erasmus in English. Professor T. S. K. Scott-Craig of Hobart College, an approved Erasmian, gave me a number of suggestions. My colleague, Professor Paul Coleman-Norton, has assisted me with puzzling passages in the Latin. For the quotation from Aristotle's *Rhetoric* in my essay I draw upon the translation by Professor Lane Cooper.

This, I sincerely hope, is Erasmus's book. The only justification for a new version is that the others represent Erasmus, to a modern reader, less adequately than is desirable or possible. Since it is his, I do not dedicate it; but my labors upon it may be inscribed: *Ad laudem uxoris meae duumque filiorum nostrorum, qui stultitiam meam toleraverunt, riserunt, atque interdum* (Deo gratias) *participaverunt.*

H. H. H.

Princeton, New Jersey

Contents

THE FOLLY OF ERASMUS: AN ESSAY xi

PREFACE: DESIDERIUS ERASMUS TO HIS FRIEND

    THOMAS MORE 1

MORIAE ENCOMIUM, THAT IS, THE PRAISE OF FOLLY 7

ANALYSIS 129

NOTES 143

INDEX OF PROPER NAMES 155

THE FOLLY OF ERASMUS

The Folly of Erasmus

THROUGH MORE THAN FOUR CENTURIES THE
world has found this book useful. As with so
many good things, those who have had most
need for it have failed to use it. But as also
with many great books, beyond its audience
of readers has extended a wide fringe of influence, within
which have stood the many who have known that such a
book existed, have known, too, that there was something
electric in it and that its author transmitted through it, as
he did through other of his labors, a spirit whose working
sends our minds at once to the parable of the Gospels:

> Whereunto shall I liken the kingdom of God? It is like
> leaven, which a woman took and hid in three measures
> of meal, till the whole was leavened.

Yet while this points to the subtle nature of the Erasmian
force, and to its manner of diffusion, this gives no account
of its direction or content, unless we make bold to press
the citation and associate the spirit in question with the
kingdom of the parable. We can say, with understate-
ment, that Erasmus is not far from the kingdom; yet to
define this last has perplexed our divines. We may hope,
with Erasmus, that it is one of the mysteries revealed to
the simple and foolish.

Cataloguers put *The Praise of Folly* on the shelf of satire,
and with reason; yet we do wrong to make this classifica-
tion too casually or too absolutely. Satire is directed at an
object, or at objects, within the actual view of the satirist.

Thus Erasmus makes ridiculous the dishonest and irreligious monks who infested some of the orders. He attacks, both by analysis and by parody, the methods of Biblical interpretation used by scholastics, or by interpreters without Greek or Hebrew. But the vitality of the book does not lie in these jibes or attacks. It owes far more to the comprehensive irony which informs these and other passages where he is pleading, ever so obliquely, for tolerance, for an understanding of human nature, for light on the dark areas of man's world. If the book were, as some have seemed to consider it, an unbroken series of satirical comments, unless it had a positive spirit greater than the keenness or deftness or disinfectant power of these, we could not read it at this late time with edification.

The point seems to be that satirists rarely destroy or appreciably correct the obliquities they attack. If they did, their works would be dull reading indeed. And why should satirists of our time still be shooting at the butts used by Aristophanes, Juvenal, Lucian, and Cervantes? A satirist may succeed in making a person ridiculous, but that is a narrow success which gives him no great claim upon the regard of mankind, particularly of posterity. The real power of great satirists is positive rather than negative. They attract, if at all, by some steady light which burns in them, a light that is benevolent and grateful to the reader—yes, even in Swift, where the style surely rests and invites the spirit as well as the eye. Swift has much humor, as well—another blessing without bitterness. The great satirist lifts the reader to his own plane of clear vision, and wins confidence by reposing in the reader confidence that this vision will be shared. Good satire is an intrigue among honest men, a conspiracy of the candid. But intriguing and conspiring, with a little change of scale, become statesmanship. To return, then, the spirit of Erasmus shows itself in its full power not in overt or direct satire, but rather in overlays of irony and in the positive drive of the whole construction of this eloquent, humane, and finely concatenated speech put in the mouth of Folly. When it is added up, the sum may as well be called criticism as satire. Mary Colum has lately said of criticism that "as an intellectual force it represents a principle through which the world of ideas renews itself, which prunes and trims old ideas to satisfy new ideas and aspirations." Does not *The Praise of Folly* do just this? It is not an irrelevance to notice that this book had been circulating for eighty years in Latin and forty years in English when Shakespeare began to write.

Mrs. Colum goes on: "Purely literary criticism . . . represents, in the work of its highest practitioners, that branch of literature whose most important office is the originating of ideas, the discovery of the circumstances, the foreseeing of the lines that other branches of literature follow." Erasmus does not do all this, and certainly he is not writing purely literary criticism. And yet—there is an old "critical problem" concerning the relation of art and morality, or of art and truth, though the shorter and uglier word may change the problem somewhat. Recently the question has involved art and propaganda; and critics have sought to dissociate the two, to justify or to condemn their copresence, to set up art as pure form, or to transcend the distinction in some other way. In *The*

Praise of Folly, one might say, Erasmus did not consider this or any related question. Yet he contributed to thought upon the subject and helped determine the practice of the sixteenth and of later centuries. With him the problem took the form of the relation of classical art, classical poetry and mythology in particular, to the Christian doctrine and life. Can anyone who reads this book doubt where he stands? Yet he never talks about the matter except to make fun, in good Lucianic fashion, of "the gods of the poets," to utter burlesque invocations to the Muses, to speak of Horace (in Horace's own words, to be sure) as "that fat sleek hog from the sty of Epicurus," to call Homer "the father of nonsense," and to quote him in very trivial connections. He was revealing, not stating, that poetry may be read and enjoyed without being treated either as an insidious intoxicant or as the vehicle of sacrosanct wisdom, and that the better a person knows poetry the more fun he can have with it. The reader is aware, long before laying down the book, that Erasmus cares deeply for classical poetry, and that he believes a Christian will be better off for knowing Greek—though he also believes that among unlettered folk will be found some of the best and most admirable Christians. Since both beliefs appear to be borne out by observation, Erasmus may not have been wrong, though the flat statement sounds paradoxical.

How did this subtle and complex construction come into being? Let us begin with the document. Μωρίας Εγκώμιον, Erasmus's own title for it, became in Latinized Greek *Moriae Encomium*, and in Latin *Stultitiae Laus*. It would have been more accurate and informing if our early translators had closely followed the Greek and had brought the book into English as "Folly's Eulogy," or "The Panegyric of Folly." An encomium (or encomion) is a eulogy or panegyric, a species of the genus oration. It is a set speech giving and asking praise of its subject, and in the orthodox tradition of serious rhetoric its subject is a person, living or dead. A rhetorical game grew up, as we may learn from Erasmus himself, in which one might compose a eulogy of one of the gods, of a character in Homer, or even of the ass; one might pronounce a panegyric upon baldness, or write in praise of darkness, or of nothing. Erasmus also refers to this work as a "declamation," another rhetorical term, with the special suggestion that the speech was thought of as an academic one, or as a "show piece," for no particular occasion. Since the audience is once addressed as *Viri*, and the speaker is wearing an academic gown, we are led to think that Erasmus had in mind a gathering in a college hall, before which a "senior sophister," or even a distinguished visiting scholar, might well appear with a learned declamation.

The topics for composing a eulogy upon a man were set forth in the standard books of instruction for speakers and writers, beginning with Aristotle's *Rhetoric*. The doctrine was that the speaker should begin with a man's ancestry and family, and find something notable there; perhaps even the country or city of his birth would lend evidence of his merit; his upbringing and education would be canvassed for similar evidence; and then one passed on to his achievements, his virtues, his public honors, and so on. Somewhere along the line, the speaker might magnify the man's friends and associates, or the people who served him, in order to borrow thence some glory. Each circumstance was not only mentioned but also amplified—aggravated, if you like. Thus if a man was descended from kings or nobles, of course he partook of their noble and royal qualities; if he came of humble stock, his own virtue was the greater for having climbed above the common run without the advantage of high birth. If one eulogized, as a *jeu d'esprit*, such a thing as mud (and *Luti Encomium* by M. Antonius Majoragius is extant), one might treat the matter of parentage fancifully, saying that the parents of mud are those two most serviceable and ancient of all creatures, water and earth. All of this lore, the reader of *The Praise of Folly* finds, was known to Erasmus and put to use by Folly.

There are other traditions lying back of the book and flowing through it to modern times. They belong in our picture, however briefly they must be dismissed here. One is the tradition of "fool literature," of which the great seamark is the *Narrenschiff*—"Ship of Fools"—which Sebastian Brant, a Strasburg inn-keeper's son who had become a learned lawyer, composed in his native Swabian dialect and published in 1494. In easy verses Brant characterizes 112 kinds of fools who journeyed aboard his imagined ship. *Narrenschiff* became *Stultifera Navis* when it was translated into Latin in 1497, and thus it circulated widely through Europe. Then Badius Ascensius, a Flemish friend of Erasmus's, believing that Brant had not allowed enough women on board his boat, wrote an enlarged version, with six more ships provided for female fools. This work by Badius was in Latin, but it was translated into French at once by a translator who further enlarged it. And so it went. *Narrenschiff* came to people who could read only English in two versions published in the same

year, 1509. One, a prose rendering of the French enlargement of Badius's translation and enlargement of Brant,
was made by a young man named Henry Watson. The
other, more successful and more widely read, was Alexander Barclay's *Ship of Folys of the World*, "translated out
of Laten, Frenche and Doche." This is rhymed in very
halting verses and stanzas, and by its author's own
avowal keeps no close adherence to any of his several
originals. Barclay had discovered some fools in England
who fell under none of the many classes described by
Continental authorities upon the subject.

At any rate, it is interesting to remember that while
Erasmus, who knew his Brant in Latin and perhaps in
one or two other tongues as well, rode over the Alps from
Italy, meditating upon folly, and while at the house of
Thomas More, suffering from lumbago, he wrote out the
fruits of his meditation, Henry Watson and Alexander
Barclay were also engrossed with their own compilations
upon the same subject. The presses of Henry Pynson and
Wynkyn de Worde in London were thumping, proof was
being read, printers were justifying forms and hanging
up freshly-printed sheets to dry—all occupied with folly.
Erasmus's own book was put into type two years later,
1511, and captivated literate Europe.

A still more important influence in shaping this book
was a favorite author of Erasmus's, Lucian. We need learn
no other names for this great humorist, since he has come
down as plain Lucian, though sometimes given the addition, "of Samasota," the town on the Euphrates river
where he was born. He was a Syrian of late Rome, dying
about A.D. 200, and so much the cosmopolitan that he
seems never to have stayed long in one place, but knew

the cities of Asia Minor, Greece, Italy, Egypt, and even Gaul. He left some eighty-five works in Greek prose, mostly short and in the form of eulogies, lectures, monologues, essays, narratives, and, above all, dialogues. The world knows best his *Dialogues of the Gods*, *Dialogues of Courtesans*, and *Dialogues of the Dead;* and possibly with these should be named his *True History*, an account of his travels "from the Pillars of Hercules into the Western Ocean," including a visit to Elysium and conversations with the shades of philosophers and heroes, the whole a parody of the old historians, travel-writers, and poets. Lucian also wrote the story of the golden ass, which we know better in the telling of Apuleius, his contemporary. Almost every sort of literary treatment except the orthodox poetic one of idealized representation we find in Lucian. From what is nowadays called "stark realism" through scurrility, irony, burlesque, parody, satire, the mock-heroic, to fantasy, here is God's plenty.

Lucian was a favorite with men of the Renaissance, and six of his dialogues had been put into type at Rome in or by 1472. There were thirty-five publications of parts of his work, either in the original or translated into Latin, before 1500. Aldus issued his *Opera* at Venice in 1503, with a title-page bearing four lines in Greek, "Lucian to his Book," which have been translated thus:

> These are the works of Lucian, who knew that folly is of ancient birth, and that what seems wise to some men appears ridiculous to others; there is no common judgment in men, but what you admire others will laugh at.

These are sentiments we find expressed also by Erasmus's Folly. By 1505 Erasmus and Thomas More, who may have discovered this author before Erasmus did, were at work translating dialogues by Lucian into Latin, and thirty-two of their versions (of which twenty-eight were by Erasmus) were printed by Badius in Paris, 1506. On the title-page of this work by an ancient scoffer it was recorded that the translator was *nuper sacri theologiae laurea decorato*, that is, Erasmus had "recently been honored with the degree of Doctor of Sacred Theology" by the University of Turin.

Later Erasmus was to publish translations of seven more pieces by Lucian, and to write his own colloquies, some of which follow closely the models set by the old Syrian. But enough has been said, though more is available, to prove him a Lucianist. Some years after he had published *The Praise of Folly* he wrote to a friend that it was Thomas More's fondness for wit and fun, "and especially for Lucian," that prompted him to write this book. The early part is Lucianic in its scoffing at the gods of mythology; and farther on Erasmus borrows from Lucian the view of the world as seen from heaven or from a great height, the world compared to a stage, and other devices. The reader who has not had time for Lucian may yet encounter here, and probably enjoy, the Lucianic irony. It is less obviously benevolent than Socratic irony. It is likely to hold itself, as well as other things, lightly. It cuts more than one way. The reader may also catch something of Lucian's bounteous fluency, his comprehensiveness, by virtue of which he seems to be driving several horses at once, but seems also to miss nothing of the landscape or the crowd through which he drives. He is likely to be joking or emitting puns to boot. This quality we know better, perhaps, in Rabelais, who was both a Lucianist and an Erasmian.

From all the Lucianic bounty we might single out one somewhat submerged detail, which we may call "learned parody." Not in Lucian alone, but everywhere in the body of classical and modern literature, we find fun generated out of the very modes and techniques of learning itself. This fun cannot be made by one who is himself innocent of scholarship. It is no game for either the plain, blunt man or the literary dilettante. The audience, too, must have had some converse with the learned world. The author must have gone far enough in some discipline to handle easily the technical terms and to pursue the most highly approved methods, even though he intends to pursue them *ad absurdum* as rapidly as possible. Some beginning of this kind of thing we find in Aristophanes; another sort of beginning we find among the Sophists, but they sought admiration rather than amusement or satire when they composed elaborate and closely-knit arguments in support of paradoxes, or worse. They could "make the worse appear the better cause" and were proud to show off their ability. Readers of Plato's *Phaedrus* have encountered *tours de force* of this kind. Then through the mock-eulogies we have spoken of, and Lucianic burlesque, we arrive at the learned parody of the Renaissance in such a work as *The Praise of Folly* or *The Epistles of Obscure Men* (1516-17), though this last uses other modes as well and is by way of being a hoax. From a later age we get that excellent specimen, *The Art of Sinking* (1728) by Pope or by Pope and his friends. Even Lamb's "Dissertation upon Roast Pig" partakes of this tradition.

INVOLUTED PARODY

One device which cannot be dissociated from learned parody is the turning of a method or practice against itself. Thus Bishop John Jewel, the chief ornament of the English church before Hooker, as a young university lecturer composed and delivered an oration against rhetoric in which he exemplified rhetorical figures and modes in the course of ridiculing their use. Ben Jonson wrote "A Fit of Rhyme against Rhyme." We find this device in Erasmus, of course. Early in the eulogy he begins sprinkling in Greek words and phrases, and continues doing so to the end. But also early in it he singles out as one of the bad habits of modern rhetoricians this sprinkling of Greek words and phrases in their Latin compositions; he admits that he copies them. They do so, he says, to show that they are bilingual—a distinction shared by the horse-leech. They also seek to confuse and overawe their readers. Then he goes on with the practice. He scoffs at modern authors for using cryptic words, usually in a foreign tongue, as titles of their books; yet his own book bears two words of Greek as a title. But an account of all his devices of learned parody would summarize much of the book; and the topic leads to larger considerations of scholarly self-consciousness and self-criticism which belong with our final estimate of the Erasmian spirit.

A closer study of what literature Erasmus had freshly in mind when Folly began speaking would bring us to Aristophanes and Horace. The running battle she maintains with the Stoics had a model in Horace's satires and epistles. Much of the middle third of *The Praise of Folly* seems to have been suggested by Satire II, iii, which Pope later drew upon. The perfect wise man of the Stoics (Section 14) appears briefly at the end of Horace's first epistle. These details we cannot pursue. As an influence of a different sort, however, we must mention Erasmus's interest in the verities of Christian doctrine, his belief that the church had fallen away from the mind of its founder and early apostles. With this zeal for what he called "the philosophy of Christ" went an acceptance, in some measure, of the Christianized Platonism which had been arrived at by some of the Italian thinkers of the preceding generation. These modes of thought and feeling had already manifested themselves in England, to bear fruit especially in the teaching and preaching of John Colet, Dean of St. Paul's, whom both Erasmus and More admired. Thus as he rode from Italy and thought about England, it was not folly alone that engaged his mind, or his happy remembrance of the facetious Thomas More; it was also his deepest fears and hopes, his most serious thoughts, and greatest admirations, connected with religion and learning.

Let us get back to the document. Folly appears in the pulpit, a young woman, as Holbein saw her, fresh and piquant. She wears the gown of a scholar but her own cap, which has two long peaks so placed and shaped as to suggest that they are designed to cover ass's ears, and each ending in a knob—the bells of the jester. She begins a eulogy of herself, complaining at the ingratitude which men have shown; for while they have eulogized trivial objects and bad men, not one has had the grace to eulogize Folly, to whom they owe so much. Well, blow your own horn, she says, if no one will blow it for you. She knows she is good. Every circumstance—her parentage, her birthplace, her companions, the effects of her presence, the sorry spectacle of the wise men who shun her, the happiness of fools, the power she wields—everything conduces to enhance her attractions and magnify her greatness. She turns to show how different classes of men, and all women, depend upon folly for their happiness. The reader is swept along. He has seen something of the follies of the world, and recognizes the portraits. This is not mere fooling. Again and again Folly scores a palpable hit.

One has an uneasy consciousness, to be sure, that she is breaking the rules. She takes special advantage of the fact that some words have two or more meanings; and when they do not have two meanings, in the stricter sense, they have two or more sets of connotations, and Folly knows how to skip among these, cutting across lots and leaving heads in a whirl. "There's nothing either good or bad, but thinking makes it so." Folly said it before Shakespeare, in her own way; she said that there is no truth of things, but only opinions about them. Aristotle had gravely set down in his *Rhetoric* this advice to the eulogist:

> For the purposes of praise or blame, the speaker may identify a man's actual qualities with qualities bordering on them. Thus a cautious man may be represented as cold and designing, a simpleton as good-natured, a callous man as easy-going. And so in each case we may substitute one of the collateral terms, always leaning toward the best; terming the choleric and passionate man, for instance, a plain-dealer, and the arrogant man superb and dignified. . . . Thus the rash man may be described as courageous, and the spendthrift as liberal; for so it will seem to the crowd, and meanwhile a false inference can be drawn from the man's motive.

Folly knows this device, whether to use it or to expose it. The proverbs of the folk are at her tongue's end, and all seem to favor her. She also knows the approved method of literary and Biblical exegesis. Homer, Horace, and Cicero are on her side. But lest among Christians these authors have no credit, she also shows from Holy Writ that folly is honorable. Solomon and St. Paul are her best witnesses. David, Jeremiah, and Ecclesiasticus have dropped expressions which she can interpret to her purpose. Even our Lord seemed to favor the simple as against those the world calls wise. His followers are not ashamed to be called sheep, and the constant practice of the Holy Scriptures is to draw metaphors from the more innocent and perhaps more foolish animals.

Along with her equivocations, her absurdities, her high selectivity, Folly offers much that is straight satire of what the reader is glad to see satirized. Worse than this, more disturbing, that is, to one who is under the illusion that the book is the *jeu d'esprit* it pretends to be, Folly again and again talks the soundest of sense or shows a flash of poetic insight that goes beyond what even the best of good sense can ordinarily compass. The power of illusion to enhance daily life, the strength of meekness and the beauty of humility, the sadness of the human lot—these are realized in symbols or illuminated by an oblique light. As with other great books, this seems to be many books. Carlyle's "clothes philosophy" is here. Strip the clothes from the actors, says Folly, and there will be no play. See the contradiction between the king's clothes, crown, and sceptre, and the man whom they disguise. Thackeray's *Book of Snobs* is suggested, as is Bunyan's picture of Vanity Fair. Pope's clear assertion of man's duty to remain in his station and to study what is proper to him is here also. The animals are happy, says Folly, because each follows his proper nature; man alone attempts the preposterous.

Mark Twain's "poor damned human race" is very much here. Sir William Temple wrote a good sentence: "When all is done, humane life is, at the greatest and the best, but like a froward child, that must be played with and humoured a little to keep it quiet, till it falls asleep, and then the care is over." Folly said as much in several ways, and at times with almost the same cadence. Something of Rabelais is in the book; something of Swift. "The man from Mars," who sees life on earth clearly and speaks the inconvenient truth about it, is here; Folly calls him "a man dropped down from the sky." The method of Defoe's *Shortest Way with Dissenters* is the method of Folly, or at least of Erasmus. We have, in a word, a compendium of satires and comedies, with no one of them developed at full length.

Not even the figure of Folly is consistently or clearly imagined. An author who was more of a poet than Erasmus would have given her at once more depth, definition, and integrity. As one scholar has observed, in the early part of the speech she seems to be the wicked folly of Christian and Hebrew morality; farther on she embodies a conception gained from the good-natured but shrewd fool of the courts; and finally (though not in the peroration) she becomes Christian folly, a conception having kinship with the tradition and doctrine of St. Francis of Assisi. Holbein's rosy demoiselle is an inadequate figure, and could not possibly have delivered this speech. Interestingly enough, the engraver for the Leyden edition (1703) changed the face and figure, making Folly middle-aged and somewhat battered in appearance. We may know a great deal about folly when we finish the book, but we should not recognize Folly if we met her on the street. Many a reader, too, has gone over *The Praise of Folly* in an edition without Holbein's sketches and has never even pictured the goddess at the desk or the fools gaping at her discourse. Translators have blurred the small amount of dramatic circumstance which is provided. And while a feigned speech is as much a piece of fiction as any other feigned action, a book like this, which is nothing but a speech, can hardly be completely poetic. That it is a public address, constructed on obvious rhetorical lines, harms it as a poetic or fictional creation. "Dramatic monologues" as poets write them give more of the interior of their speakers, and take their form, too, from an inner necessity of character and its expression.

Yet although Erasmus was an imperfect dramatist, he was, as has been suggested, a great critic. The mordant power of this book is his own, elevated and caught at the top of its form. With all his faults, his cowardice, some would say, and his exhibitions of pettiness—but these are not so many as the phrase suggests—Erasmus seems to have maintained a consistency in his work and life, so that these join to display a spirit which has given heart and hope to his colleagues in scholarship, to all the liberal-minded, in fact, in all countries and in all times since his own. One who does no more than read this one little book of his finds that broad statement credible. Yet it is an easy book to misread. And one leading suggestion of the pages which follow is that while *The Praise of Folly* is an authentic expression of the essential Erasmian spirit, we do wrong to take Folly herself as the author's accredited representative, except in a few passages—and in those he rather forgets that Folly is speaking.

A PROBLEM IN READING

To make clearer this apparently confused view is a nice problem in literary interpretation. We may be helped by analyzing another, more familiar, problem in the same field. Consider the farewell speech of Polonius to Laertes in *Hamlet*—the "few precepts" which the young man going away to the University is to remember. "Be thou familiar, but by no means vulgar." "Give every man thine ear, but few thy voice." "Neither a borrower nor a lender be." And so on, up to this pitch:

> This above all: to thine own self be true;
> And it must follow, as the night the day,
> Thou canst not then be false to any man.

This has been read by millions, and the reading of it, or the effect of it, has varied considerably. Let us suppose that one reader believes that good literature is full of well-phrased sentiments which may be of profit to life and conduct. He will take the speech much as we imagine Polonius hoped Laertes would take it. He believes it, in other words, partly because it sounds like good sense, partly because the spectacle of an aged father saying farewell to his son breaks down or prevents resistance to belief, partly because, knowing Shakespeare to be a great author, the reader infers that what he writes in the form of direct advice will be sound. This reader may even go so far as to quote the concluding three lines in moral exhortations. In general, he ignores entirely the dramatic form of *Hamlet;* if he is conscious of it, he may take the position that even a character in a play may express valuable truths.

For our second reader, let us take one at an opposite extreme. This one knows something about Shakespeare and the history of the stage and of literature. He judges, from other circumstances of the play, that Shakespeare did not intend Polonius to seem wise or prudent but rather as senile and slightly foolish. Hamlet himself seems to take this view. This reader knows that Shakespeare frequently parodied or satirized common literary or dramatic conventions. In *Midsummer Night's Dream* he burlesqued plays put on by groups of tradesmen. So this reader decides that here Shakespeare is making fun of the whole matter of a father's advice to his son, and he reads Polonius's speech as a parody on such farewell speeches, but one which might well have been produced by such a doting old gaffer as Polonius. He does not believe the speech at all, but he believes it is consistent with the character of Polonius and with the purpose of the dramatist. This is a highly sophisticated reading, just as the first reader's was a naïve one.

A third reader may also find the speech proper to the character of Polonius, but he may judge that since the speaker is represented as being the principal counsellor of the king of Denmark and with much experience of life, he is not altogether a fool; his speech will show some shrewdness, some worldly wisdom, some pompousness and windiness, perhaps; but it is by no means a burlesque of such things. This interpreter will not take it seriously as a guide of life, though he may find sayings in it which seem to hit off with great exactness what appear to be sound rules of conduct. This reader is sophisticated also, but in this interpretation he might be called primarily reasonable.

Yet it is possible to conceive of a reader who stands on another level of reading entirely, a level on which the attitude toward this particular speech becomes a very minor matter. We might call the interpretation at this level a concrete one, by way of distinguishing it from all the others, which alike tended to be abstract. Our fourth reader (though any other, by grace or discipline, may also stand on this level) is likely not to give any interpretation to this particular speech except while he reads, or just after he reads, the entire play. He finds the whole not only more important than the parts, but also more absorbing. He arrives at his conception of the whole, you may say, by reading or hearing the parts, perhaps also by the use of much commentary and analysis. Even so, once the conception is present, his reading of any particular speech is always tangential to or conditional upon it. It is not merely an intellectual structure, to be diagrammed and fixed, but it is experiential. That is the reason he wishes to go over the whole before discussing this speech. Sophistication, or the control of attitudes by a purposive manipulation of somewhat isolated pieces of knowledge, gives way to imagination, which works to fuse all experience—even the experience of being sophisticated and that of being reasonable—into a unity. Our reader sees the play, it must be, as a world, a universe, to be entered. Much as he may like to enter it, he cannot very well carry pieces out of it. Of what we ordinarily call the universe, whose form and limits, whose oneness, even, we cannot see, we usually say that we might understand the whole if we could fully understand a single object in it. Yet this would be true only if we had a sense of the whole, or of wholeness, to begin with. The world given us in a poetic work has the great advantage that it presents this sense of wholeness vividly. Just how particular persons who read concretely would interpret Polonius's speech, these brief remarks do not divulge. To go on in this direction would be to write an essay on *Hamlet*.

The example serves to show varieties and levels of interpretation. Remembering that *The Praise of Folly* is not a consummated poetic fiction, we cannot look to it for a world of its own; yet an interesting analogy will appear, and here also we must strive toward a concrete reading. Some keys to interpretation are plainly inadequate. This might be suggested, for instance: since Erasmus puts his discourse in the mouth of Folly, he intends it all to be foolishness; none of it is to be taken seriously, except as a dramatic presentation of what is foolish. This would indeed result in a naïve reading, and anyone capable of reading the book at all finds at once that the key does not fit. There is almost no straight or mere foolishness in it. Folly may be arguing that as a baby she was better off than was Jupiter as a baby, for he was nursed by a she-goat, whereas she was nursed by two lovely nymphs, Drunkenness and Idleness; but she presents this in beautifully correct sentences in its exact place in a well-planned progression. Farther along, when she tells the duties of a king and the dangers of his position, she talks as gravely as any philosopher. We look for a better key. We know the proverb, as does Folly, "Children and fools sometimes speak the truth." This suggests that while there will be nonsense in the oration, there will be flashes of wisdom, much as we find in the parts of the fools in Shakespeare. There are such flashes, but the whole is not to be described in this manner. There are wholly grave sections of considerable length, suggesting Shakespeare's kings and counsellors rather than his fools. There is learned parody, and serious Biblical criticism. Above all, there is a beautiful orderliness and a rising movement quite inconsistent with mere deviation into sense.

Folly herself offers another help toward our interpretation. Referring (in Section 13) to Plato's *Symposium*, she recalls that Alcibiades drew an analogy from the little images of Silenus current at the time, which were ugly when looked at, but which, when opened, were found to contain beautifully carved images of the gods. Folly tells us that we must not be content with the appearances of things but must look for the true interior meaning. (This is inconsistent with what she says elsewhere about the supremacy of opinion, but let that pass.) Pressing this suggestion to the limit, we might be led to say that Erasmus intends Folly really to represent Wisdom. The nonsense or fooling she indulges in, then, is but superficial disguise or a relish, a kind of unbending proper to a wise person. Folly thus becomes a completely "sympathetic" figure, and she has sometimes been so interpreted. Such a key seems more serviceable, indeed, than the others we have tried. Falstaff is a complex character whom we view with mingled emotions but whom, on the whole, we may find sympathetic. We might similarly overlook the inconsistencies of Folly, her suppression of facts—for she rarely dwells upon the consequences of folly—and her defense of bad causes, for the sake of her hatred of pretense, her occasional sweet reasonableness, and her broad sympathies. The main difficulties with the view are that it claims for Folly a consistency which, as has been pointed out, does not exist, and for Erasmus a power of dramatic conception which was denied him. Were Folly really integrated into a character such as this view calls for, she would stand with the few great figures of comic creation in the world's literature. In her own right, as character, she does not so stand. At times she seems to be on the way to become a character; but usually she is a puppet, and at times is forgotten completely by author and reader. So we come back to a divergence between Folly and the book, or between Folly and the author, and say that a concrete reading will involve Erasmus as well as Folly, and even more than Folly.

Both in the author's preface to Thomas More and in the declamation we find stress laid upon the notion that only fools have the privilege of speaking truth without offense. This observation, if dwelt upon, does cut deep into the motives and methods of Erasmus. He has found a device whereby he may say what he wishes to say, speak the truth as he sees it, and still plead immunity. Yet he cannot speak this truth all of the time, or no one will believe it is Folly who is before him. Following this lead, we do well to think of irony. The very writing and issuance of this book was an act of irony on the part of an eminent scholar. He was playfully ironical in connecting it as he did with Thomas More. He was ironical in another way when he said that some people hope to become rich by praying to Erasmus. He was ironical in still another way when he ridiculed the foolish love of fame which keeps scholars at their labors.

Suppose we now premise that Erasmus wishes to show that what is usually accepted as wisdom is not very wise. He will do so by placing much of it in the mouth of Folly; but along with this he will put other sentiments which are either below or above the level of ordinary wisdom— for to mundane common sense, what goes beyond or above itself is sheer folly, no less than what falls short of it. The sentiments below the ordinary level will serve to authenticate the speaker as Folly, will provide mirth, and will have a cajoling effect upon the reader, tending to break down categorical boundaries in his mind and to leave him unguarded against other kinds of attack. Sentiments above the ordinary level will be so played up as to emphasize the mediocre nature of worldly wisdom, and will be insinuated into the reader's mind with a novel attractiveness. There is something of an argument *a fortiori* here: if Folly can be as wise as this, what ought wisdom be? Or put more ironically, what men will not accept from the Evangelists and the apostles they will perhaps accept from Folly. We have a key which seems to operate throughout our reading of the eulogy, most of which can be arranged under a scheme based upon this explanation. There will be eddies within the main current, as when Folly herself uses the device of irony with a basis, or fulcrum, in either her own foolishness or her own wisdom, distinguishable from the basis of Erasmus himself. Other eddies will result from mere play of fancy. Yet something is still left over, unexplained by this key, too— principally the gusto, abandon, and joyous release which supply so much of the book's appeal, and perhaps a great part of its real message. The experience of a concrete reading will include the impact of energies as well as the shifting of attitudes and the savor of various kinds of wisdom.

It is time to look again at the document. An interesting passage (Section 17) argues that halfwits and "naturals" such as kings and noblemen used to employ as jesters are really the happiest of men. They are free, says Folly, from tortures of conscience and from fear of death. They play all of the time, and laugh a great deal. Every man, even the coldest, has a soft spot in his heart for these poor souls —except that we must not call them "poor"; Folly does not, but paints them as rich and fortunate. Her position does not represent the wisdom of the world, which may be indulgent toward these innocents but certainly reckons them among the unfortunate. Is what Folly says, then, something less than the wisdom of the world, or more? Taken as a bare argument, it is less. Such halfwits and imbeciles, as Erasmus must have known, have miseries too deep for telling. Even the best of men (such as Thomas More, who had a great liking for natural fools and kept one in his household), though they may be amused or interested by the spectacle of such people, are likely at the same time to feel a kind of pity so deep as to be painful. Others feel mere revulsion. The argument Folly makes, in a word, ignores important facts. But suppose we think of it as being the vehicle for something else, a plea for a sympathetic and understanding attitude toward these unfortunates. Then, we might say, the passage rises above worldly wisdom. It owes something to an old identification of harmless insanity with a sort of possession by divine force. But there is a tenderness in it, such as reminds us of Pope's verses about the poor Indian. Erasmus may be saying what may need to be said, that these dim-sighted souls are human souls and belong within the range of human as well as divine love. "After a life lived out in much jollity," he writes of the halfwits, "with no fear of death, or sense of it, they go straight to the Elysian fields, there to entertain the pious and idle shades with their jests." Erasmus reminds us elsewhere, too, that we are all touched, or liable to be touched, by weakness of mind.

Again, Folly draws in the sharpest of lines the picture of the deluded scholar, seeking to win a vain sort of fame by labors which with the best success in the world can but please a handful of blear-eyed scholars like himself. As a matter of fact, she sets such a man against her happy half-wit for contrast:

> Fancy some pattern of wisdom to put up against him, a man who wore out his whole boyhood and youth in pursuing the learned disciplines. He wasted the best time of life in unintermitted watchings, cares, and studies; and through the remaining part of it he never tasted so much as a tittle of pleasure; always frugal, impecunious, sad, austere; unfair and strict toward himself, morose and unamiable to others; afflicted by pallor, leanness, invalidism, sore eyes, and premature old age and white hair; dying before his appointed day.

Except for the phrase, "morose and unamiable to others," that is an excellent self-portrait. Erasmus spoke from an experience that was not without bitterness. What shall we say, then? By this condemnation of scholarly devotion in the mouth of Folly, does he mean really to condemn it? If so, then why did he, after the age of forty-three at which he wrote this book, go on to perform as prodigious and exacting labors of editorial scholarship as the world has known, not only preparing what was in effect the *editio princeps* of the Greek New Testament, with his own translation, notes, and carefully wrought paraphrase, but editing also the works of St. Chrysostom, St. Jerome, and several other fathers of the church? No, what Folly says hits pretty well the wisdom of the world. Erasmus's own labors are the comment upon it. What we know from this is that he undertook those labors with a clearsighted view of the cost of them. We might even say that he was aware of the folly of them, as judged either by the wisdom of the world or by a higher sort of wisdom which reveals to every man who has it that whatever he may do is in itself vain, and dispensable, yet the soul which he throws into it and the life he builds through it are not necessarily so. Put into other terms, except God build the house, they labor in vain that build it. On the mundane level, also, we notice that the temper of Erasmus did not accord with that of Folly's despised scholar. A favorite word with him was *festivus*—festive, companionable. He refused to allow his scholarship to kill his humanity. And thus Folly's gird has point, even as used by her; the halfwit is understandably human, all too human, while the scholar may verge toward something inhuman or anti-human.

Finally, there is the whole matter of Folly's treatment of the church and of Christian doctrine. The subject is so large that we are confined to a few general observations. Erasmus lived and died as a son of the church, suspected, it is true, of heresies, and even charged with them by many intelligent churchmen. He was hated more bitterly, however, by some of the Protestant Reformers, in that while he seemed to be saying so much they agreed with, he would not take the firm, bold action they believed the hour demanded. In this book we find much that bespeaks the Reformer rather than the orthodox churchman. The truth is that one widely circulated modern edition of Kennett's translation of *The Praise of Folly* was issued by a free-thinking publisher as ammunition in his war against Christianity. In his "Publisher's Preface" he made a long quotation from Folly, beginning, "It is observable that the Christian Religion seems to have some relation to Folly, and no alliance at all with Wisdom," with pleased assent, thereby writing himself down *stultissimum*. He himself wrote: "From the serene Citadel of Truth, armed with the weapons of reason and satire, Erasmus has in this work severely bombarded the strongholds of Faith." But Erasmus, we may flatly say, was interested in defending and arming the strongholds of faith. In Folly's attacks on churchmen she does not stand at the level of worldly wisdom, which in general approves those whom she attacks. Neither, except in moments by the way, is she speaking nonsense. Every attack is precisely against following in the spiritual kingdom the standards and practices that prevail in worldly, carnal affairs. Amid all Folly's shifts and tergiversations, Erasmus never implies that Christianity has more to learn than it has to teach. From one point of view, the church's folly has been that it has gone to school to the world; from another point of view, its folly is its glory.

Yet Folly's freedom with sacred names and texts has shocked many a reverent believer; and in his own time Erasmus was coupled with Lucian as an atheistical scoffer. This freedom, however, is itself a manifestation of that *festivitas* which Erasmus found fully accordant with reverence. One does not hurt the sacred truth by citing it in the mouth of Folly so much as one hurts it by disavowing it in one's life, or using it as a pretext for actions which, though serious and grave enough, are plainly hostile to good feeling and fundamental decency. One's faith may indeed be so real, so present, and so homely that one jests with and about it, as if it were a friend or brother. Erasmus believed that Christianity could be at home in a world of culture as well as in a religious community or among fishers and mechanics. On the other hand, the man of culture would be a fool if his cultivation carried him to the point where he lost touch with the simplicities of the Gospel which are akin to the simplicities of the unlettered human heart, even to those of dumb animals. The paradox here is as inevitable as that other paradox which Folly does not quote but which underlies much of what she says: "For whosoever will save his life shall lose it; and whosoever will lose his life for my sake shall find it."

For a more complete appreciation of Erasmus himself, we need at least to read his *Colloquies* and his *Enchiridion.* Yet the present work, as we have seen with the help of little drawn from outside it, tells us much. Though it contains sad pictures of weakness and misery, it does not tell us to laugh that we may not weep; rather it tells us to weep and to laugh in humility, "as unto the Lord," with a sense of the transience of joy and tears. It suggests that there is a simplicity which embraces and transcends complexity. The divided mind, the conflict of the soul, need not be self-destructive. Although the deepest understanding may not bring such experiences to harmony, or the play of consciousness give them a musical setting, these spiritual powers can at least place them in some degree of esthetic distance and relate them intelligibly to a pattern not quite crazy. At the more customary levels of experience, this book bids us hold our convictions with some lightness, and to add grace to life. Our best work will be done in a critical spirit, which turns upon ourselves and itself the same keen gaze and feasting irony with which it views the world. We like to think that some such spirit informs our universities. But it belongs also to this spirit not to talk about itself. Perhaps too much has been said already.

Before leaving the subject, however, we must give a hearing to the other side. Rare and precious as may be this phlogiston, it is not, we are told, a fuel for the engines of action. A Chinese philosophy resulted in a static China. Academic scepticism unfits a man for the tasks of life, which call rather for the uncritical mind and unhampered will. The answer is perhaps threefold, in part a denial with counter-charge, in part an admission, and in part an amendment. A flat denial, even in part, is the weakest of these. It is indeed true, as has been pointed out, that Socrates would make a bad member of a fire department, were he to answer a fire-call by beginning a dialogue upon whether the burning house is worth saving. Yet it is also fair to say, and needs no insistence, that practical men of undivided will often make a terrible mess of what are supposed to be practical affairs, and seem to go on making such messes either until other practical men, single-minded toward other ends, halt them, or until there is an influx of the critical spirit into some party to the situation. Not every call to action is as immediately urgent as a fire-alarm; and men touched by Erasmian folly—and Abraham Lincoln was one of them—have sometimes planned and controlled and executed palpable tasks. Even Folly admits that Marcus Aurelius was a good emperor. Thomas More—and this book is his, we find, as well as Erasmus's—was a wise and active parliamentarian, diplomat, lawyer, and Lord Chancellor.

Yet we may admit that in emergencies the Erasmian sometimes cuts a poor figure. Erasmus was a pacifist, and his folly seems to unfit men for whole-hearted participation in war. If a man cannot take his place in battle-line when necessity arises, most would say, then there is something fundamentally wrong with him. It is not an adequate answer to say that he represents the civilization which the battle defends. It is not adequate to plead specialization—*non omnia possumus omnes*. It is not adequate to say that he follows the counsel of Plato, to step into a doorway when the storm grows too fierce. On the other hand, one can testify that many a man of Erasmian spirit has gone forth to fight, perhaps not whole-heartedly believing in the complete righteousness of his cause, or even of his action, yet with motives strong enough to make him as good a soldier as the next man. It is certainly possible for one to be willing to die for a cause in which one does not wholly believe. Men die for such causes every day, not always by compulsion. And if, on the other hand, an Erasmian does refuse to fight with carnal weapons, it is just as likely that his refusal, in turn, does not represent what the world would call a whole-hearted action. The relation of the Erasmian spirit to democracy is a subject in itself; but it must occur to anyone at this point that democracies, as states, have proceeded on what we have seen to be the Erasmian principle in individuals. That is, the democratic belief is that a state can exist and be strong without being totalitarian; that it can endure considerable divisions of sentiment within it, and that it can even protect the right of individual conscience without paralyzing the national will.

The concept of emergency, or crisis, comes at times to loom large in our consciousness, and with reason. Yet unless it is to swell and involve all other concepts, there is place for the Erasmian spirit; and if it so extinguishes all else, the Erasmian, at worst, will be but a little less vital than the single-minded man of action. When the Duke of Norfolk pleaded with Thomas More to go along with the Act of Supremacy, warning him that his contumacy might cost him his head, More listened patiently and then said: "Is that all, my Lord? Then in good faith there is no more difference between your Grace and me, but that I shall die today and you tomorrow."

The best in a corrupted form is the worst of all. The degraded Erasmian is the shifty, accommodating Pyrrhonist, sceptical of all except his own kind of scepticism. Irony, in him, becomes cynicism; wit becomes flippancy; and his criticism of life adds up to an avoidance of responsibility. In this he is as far from Erasmus as he is from John Wesley or Julius Caesar. In the present book, one decisive distinction between Folly and the author is that Folly is at times cynical, Erasmus is not. For the rest, what Erasmus did has somehow survived and gone on working. What men of his spirit did and said and wrote has survived to exert a modicum of force in the world. Wars, conquests, and revolutions have not quite extinguished this spirit, and have not made it seem less of a blessing.

THE · PRAISE · OF · FOLLY

Preface   –

DESIDERIUS ERASMUS OF ROTTERDAM TO THOMAS MORE,
HIS FRIEND, SALUTATIONS:

COMING OUT OF ITALY A WHILE AGO, ON MY WAY
to England, I did not want to waste in idle talk
and popular stories all the hours I had to sit on
horseback, but chose at times to think over
some topics from the studies we share in common, or to enjoy my memories of friends—and I had left
some here in England who were wholly learned and
wholly gracious. Among them you, More, came first to
mind. Thus, absent as I was, I found delight in the memory of the absent you in much the same way as, being
present, I used to enjoy the society of the present you;
and may I be shot if anything more pleasant than that
has ever befallen me in life! So because I thought that by
all means something ought to be done about it, and the
time seemed hardly suitable for serious intellectual effort,
I was pleased to have some sport with a eulogy of folly.

What goddess Pallas, you may ask, put that into my
head? First, of course, your family name of More prompted
me; which comes as near to the word for folly as you are
far from the meaning of it; by the suffrages of all, you are
as far as one can be. Then I supposed that this exercise of
wit would meet with special favor from you, because you
are wont to enjoy to the full jokes of this kind, that is,
those that are somewhat learned—perhaps I flatter myself—yet not at all heavy; and through our common

course of mortality you move as a sort of Democritus. Although, to be sure, because of a certain unique perspicacity in your make-up you are accustomed to dissent sharply from the crowd, at the same time because of your incredibly affable and easy ways you can play the man of all hours with all men, and enjoy doing so.

May you take in good will, then, this little declamation, as a keepsake from a friend, and may you also undertake to defend it; dedicated to you, it is now yours and not mine. For probably contentious fellows will turn up who will cavil, on the one part saying that these trifles are more frivolous than befits a theologian, and on the other that they are more biting than befits a meek Christian; and they will cry that we are reviving the Old Comedy or Lucian, and carping peevishly at everything. Let any, however, who are offended by the lightness and foolery of my argument remember, I beg, that mine is not the first example, but that the same thing was often practised by great authors. Homer, all those ages ago, made sport with a battle of frogs and mice; Virgil, with a gnat, and a salad; Ovid, with a nut. Polycrates eulogized Busiris; and Isocrates, though a castigator of Polycrates, did the same; Glaucon argued in praise of injustice; Favorinus, of Thersites and of the quartan fever; Synesius, of baldness; Lucian, of the fly and of the parasite. Seneca sported with an Apotheosis of the Emperor Claudius; Plutarch, in a dialogue between Gryllus and Ulysses; Lucian and Apuleius, with an ass; and someone whom I do not know, with the last will and testament of Grunius Corocotta, a hog. Saint Jerome makes mention of this last.

Well, if it pleases them, let them suppose that all this time I have been playing checkers to refresh my spirits or, if they prefer, that I have been riding a hobby-horse. For what an injustice it is, when we allow to each way of life its own recreations, that none should be permitted to studies! Especially when literary trifles may lead to serious matter, and fooleries may be so handled that a reader who is not altogether a fathead may garner more of profit from them than from the bristling and pompous arguments of some whom we know. As, for instance, one fellow praises rhetoric or philosophy in a pieced-up oration, another paints the glories of some prince, another exhorts to the end of making war against the Turks, another foretells the future; and still another works up a new set of little essays relating to—a lock of goat's-wool. Nothing is more puerile, certainly, than to treat serious matters triflingly; but nothing is more graceful than to handle light subjects in such a way that you seem to have been anything but trifling. The judgment of others upon me will be what it will be. Yet unless self-love deceives me badly, I have praised folly in a way not wholly foolish.

Now to answer that other cavil, of carping, this liberty has always been permitted to men of wit, that in their jests they may poke fun at the general manners of men with impunity, so long as their license does not extend to outrage. For this reason I wonder a little at the tenderness of ears in these times, which can tolerate nothing, almost, but solemn forms of address. Yes, you will see some so perversely religious that they can endure the broadest scoffs against Christ Himself sooner than hear a pope or a prince glanced at in the most casual sort of jest—but especially if something touching revenues is involved. Yet he that censures the lives of men in such a way that he points at no individual by name—I ask whether he does not seem to teach, and to warn, rather than to bite? Otherwise, by all that's holy, under how many topics am I taxing myself? Besides, he who spares no class of men would seem to be angry at no person, but at the vices of all. Hence if anyone turns up complaining that he has been libelled, he betrays his bad conscience or, at best, his fear. Saint Jerome indulged in this kind of writing, and with greater freedom and sharpness; sometimes he did not omit names. But aside from the fact that I refrain throughout from using names, I have in addition so tempered my style that the judicious reader will easily perceive that my end is pleasure rather than censure. I do not anywhere rake into the occult cesspool of vices, after the manner of Juvenal, but take care to set out things that are ridiculous rather than foul. Still, if there is anyone whom the work cannot please, he should at least remember this, that it is a fine thing to be slandered by Folly. Since I have feigned her speaking, it was of course necessary to preserve decorum in her character.

Yet why do I say these things to you, an advocate so distinguished that you can defend in the best way even causes not the best? Farewell, learned More, and doughtily defend your Moria.

From the Country
June 9th

MORIAE ENCOMIUM

THAT IS, THE PRAISE OF FOLLY

A DECLAMATION

BY DESIDERIUS ERASMUS

HOWEVER MORTAL FOLK MAY COMMONLY SPEAK of me (for I am not ignorant how ill the name of Folly sounds, even to the greatest fools), I am she—the only she, I may say —whose divine influence makes gods and men rejoice. One great and sufficient proof of this is that the instant I stepped up to speak to this crowded assembly, all faces at once brightened with a fresh and unwonted cheerfulness, all of you suddenly unbent your brows, and with frolic and affectionate smiles you applauded; so that as I look upon all present about me, you seem flushed with nectar, like gods in Homer, not without some nepenthe, also; whereas a moment ago you were sitting moody and depressed, as if you had come out of the cave of Trophonius. Just as it commonly happens, when the sun first shows his splendid golden face to the earth or when, after a bitter winter, young spring breathes mild west winds, that a new face comes over everything, new color and a sort of youthfulness appear; so at the mere sight of me, you straightway take on another aspect. And thus what great orators elsewhere can hardly bring about in a long, carefully planned speech, I have done in a moment, with nothing but my looks.

As to why I appear today in this unaccustomed garb, you shall now hear, if only you will not begrudge lending your ears to my discourse—not those ears, to be sure, which you carry to sermons, but those which you are accustomed to prick up for mountebanks in the market-place, for clowns and jesters, the ears which, in the old days, our friend Midas inclined to the god Pan. It is my pleasure for a little while to play the rhetorician before you, yet not one of the tribe of those who nowadays cram certain pedantic trifles into the heads of schoolboys, and teach a more than womanish obstinacy in disputing; no, I emulate those ancients who, to avoid the unpopular name of philosophers, preferred to be called Sophists. Their study was to celebrate in eulogies the virtues of gods and of heroic men. Such a eulogy, therefore, you shall hear, but not of Hercules or Solon; rather of my own self—to wit, Folly.

[2] Nor do I have any use for those wiseacres who preach that it is most foolish and insolent for a person to praise himself. Yet let it be as foolish as they would have it, if only they will grant that it is proper: and what is more suitable than that Folly herself should be the trumpeter of her praises? "She is her own flute-player." Who, indeed, could portray me better than can I myself? Unless it could so happen that I am better known to some one else than I am to myself. On the whole, however, I deem that what I am doing is much more decent than what a host of our best people, and scholars even, do continually. With a certain perverse modesty they are wont to convey instructions to some sycophantic speaker or prattling poet whom they have engaged at a fee; and then they hear back from him their praises, that is to say,

some pure fiction. The blushing listener, meanwhile, spreads his plumes like a peacock, and bridles, while the brazen adulator searches among the gods to find a parallel for this good-for-nothing, and proposes him as the complete exemplar of all virtues—from which the man himself knows that he is farther away than twice infinity. Thus the flatterer adorns a crow with other birds' feathers, washes the Ethiopian white, and, in sum, makes an elephant out of a gnat. Lastly, I follow the familiar proverb of the folk, to the effect that he rightly praises himself who never meets anyone else who will praise him. Here, by the way, I wonder at the ingratitude, or perhaps the negligence, of men: although all of them studiously cherish me and freely acknowledge my benefits, not a one has emerged so far in all the ages to celebrate the praises of Folly in a grateful oration. In the meantime, there has been no lack of those who at great expense of lamp-oil and of sleep have extolled, in elegant eulogies, Busiruses, Phalarises, quartan fevers, flies, baldness, and pests of that sort.

And now you shall hear from me an extemporaneous speech, unlabored, but so much the truer for all that. I should not want you to think it is made to show off my wit, as is done by the common run of orators. They, as you know so well, when they bring out a speech they have been working on for thirty whole years, and sometimes not their own at all, will swear it was written in three days, for pastime, or even that they merely dictated it. For my part, it has always been most satisfactory to speak "whatever pops into my head."

[3] And let no one expect that, after the manner of these ordinary orators, I shall expound myself by defini-

tion, much less divide myself. For it is equally unlucky to circumscribe with a limit her whose nature extends so universally or to dissect her in whose worship every order of being is at one. Anyway, what end would be served in setting forth by definition a sketch and, as it were, a shadow of me, when you, present here, with your own eyes perceive me in your presence? I am as you see me, that true disposer of good things whom the Latins call *Stultitia* and the Greeks Μωρία.

Still, what need was there to tell you this, as if in my very face and front, so to speak, I do not sufficiently announce who I am? As if anyone who was claiming that I am Minerva or the Spirit of Wisdom could not immediately be refuted by one good look, even if I were not speaking—though speech is the least deceptive mirror of the mind. I have no use for cosmetics. I do not feign one thing in my face while I hold something else in my heart. I am in all points so like myself that even those who specially arrogate to themselves the part and name of wise men cannot conceal me, though they walk about "like apes in scarlet or asses in lion-skins." Let them carry it as cunningly as you could ask, the protruding ears will somewhere betray the Midas. An ungrateful class of men that, so help me! Although they are wholly of my party, in public they are so ashamed of my name that they toss it up at others as a great reproach! Wherefore, since in fact they are μωρότατοι, "most foolish," and yet are eager to seem wise men and veritable Thaleses, shall we not with entire justice dub them μωροσόφους, "foolosophers"? It has seemed well, you note, to imitate the rhetoricians of our time, who believe themselves absolutely to be gods if they can show themselves bilingual (like a horse-leech), and account it a famous feat if they can weave a few Greekish words, like inlay work, ever and anon into their Latin orations, even if at the moment there is no place for them. Then if they want exotic touches, they dig four or five obsolete words out of decaying manuscripts, by which they spread darkness over the reader; with the idea, I warrant you, that those who understand will be vastly pleased with themselves, and those who do not understand will admire the more—and all the more the less they understand. The fact is that there is a rather elegant species of enjoyment among our sect, to fall into special love with what is specially imported. Some who are a little more ambitious laugh and applaud, and, by example of the ass, shake their ears, so that in the eyes of the rest they will seem to comprehend: "Quite so, quite so." Now I go back to my outline.

[4] You have my name, gentlemen . . . gentlemen . . . what shall I add by way of an epithet? What but "most foolish"? For by what more honorable style could the Goddess of Folly address her devotees? But since it is not known to very many from what stock I have sprung, I shall now attempt, with the Muses' kind help, to set this forth. Not Chaos, or Orcus, or Saturn, or Iapetus, or any other of that old-fashioned and musty set of gods, was my father at all. It was Plutus, who only, in spite of Hesiod, Homer, and Jove himself to boot, is "the father of gods and men." At a single nod of Plutus, as of old so nowadays, all things sacred and profane are turned topsy-turvy. At his pleasure, all war, peace, empires, plans, judgments, assemblies, marriages, treaties, pacts, laws, arts, sports, weighty matters (my breath is giving out)— in short, all public and private affairs of mortal men, are

governed. Without his help all that population of deities of the poets' making—nay, I speak very boldly, even those top gods—either would not exist at all or would be "diners at home," keeping house very meagrely. To the person who rouses Plutus's anger Pallas herself cannot bring help enough; on the other hand, whoever possesses his favor can bid great Jove and his thunder go hang themselves. "I glory to have such a father." And he did not procreate me out of his head, as Jupiter did that austere and homely Pallas; but rather out of Youth, the loveliest nymph of all, and the jolliest as well. Nor did he do this confined in the irksome marriage-bond—the way that blacksmith was born lame!—but indeed he did it in a much pleasanter manner, "mingled in love," as our father Homer puts it. Yet, make no mistake, it was not the Plutus of Aristophanes, already decrepit and weak in the eyes, that engendered me, but the same god healthy and as yet heated by his youth; nor by youth only, but also by nectar, which he had chanced to drink rather copiously and rather straight at a banquet of the gods.

If you are also wanting to know the place of my nativity (seeing that in these days it is accounted a prime point of nobility, in what place you uttered your first cries), I was not brought forth in floating Delos, or on the foaming sea, or "in hollow caverns," but right in the Fortunate Isles, where all things grow "without ploughing or planting." In those islands is no drudgery or old age, nor is there any sickness. In the fields one never sees a daffodil, mallow, leek, bean, or any of such kind of trash; but one's eyes and nose are enchanted at the same time by moly, panacea, nepenthes, sweet marjoram, ambrosia, lotus, rose, violet, hyacinth, and the gardens of Adonis. And being born among these delights, I did not enter upon life with weeping, but right off I laughed sweetly at my mother. Nor indeed do I envy great Jupiter his nurse, a she-goat, since two charming nymphs nourished me at their breasts—Drunkenness, offspring of Bacchus, and Ignorance, Pan's daughter.

These two you see here in the company of my other attendants and followers. If you wish to know all their names, you will not hear them from me, so help me, except in Greek. This one whom you observe here, with the eyebrows haughtily raised, is Philautia. She with the smiling eyes, so to speak, whom you see clapping her hands, is named Kolakia. The one who is half asleep, and like a drowsy person, is called Lethe. She that leans on her elbows, with her hands folded, is Misoponia. Hedone is the one wearing the rosy wreath and smelling of perfumes. The lady with the uncertain eyes rolling here and there is called Anoia; and she with the glistening skin and body in good point is Tryphe. You see also two male gods among the girls, one of whom they call Comus, the other Negretos Hypnos. These, I say, are my household servants, with whose faithful help I bring every sort of thing under my rule, maintaining my empire even over emperors.

[5] You have learned of my family, upbringing, and companions. Now, that it may not look as if I have usurped the name of goddess for myself without good grounds, please give closest attention while I tell how many advantages I bestow on both gods and men, and how broadly my power is displayed. For if, as some one has judiciously observed, this only is to be a god, to help men, and if deservedly they have been admitted to the

rank of gods who have shown to mortals the use of wine, or grain, or any other such commodity, why am not I of right named and venerated as the *alpha* of all gods, who single-handed bestow all things on all men?

In the first place, what can be dearer or more precious than life? And the beginning and first principle of life is owed to whom else but me? Not the spear of "potent-fathered" Pallas, not the shield of "cloud-compelling" Jove, procreates the children of men or multiplies their race. Even he, the father of gods and king of men, who shakes all heaven by a nod, is obliged to lay aside his three-pronged thunder and that Titanic aspect by which, when he pleases, he scares all the gods, and assume another character in the slavish manner of an actor, if he wishes to do what he never refrains from doing, that is to say, to beget children. Now the Stoics believe that they are next-door neighbors to gods. But give me a triple Stoic, or a quadruple one, or, if you will, a Stoic multiplied by six hundred; if for this purpose he will not put off his beard, the ensign of wisdom (though displayed also by goats), yet he will certainly lay by his gravity, smooth his brow, renounce his rock-bound principles, and for a few minutes toy and talk nonsense. In fine, the wise man must send for me, I repeat, if he ever wishes to become a father. And why not speak to you still more frankly, as is my fashion? I beg to inquire whether the head, whether the face, the breast, the hand, or the ear—all of them accounted honorable members—generates gods and men? I judge not; nay, rather that foolish, even silly, part which cannot be named without laughter, is the propagator of the human race. This is at last that sacred spring from which all things derive existence, more truly than from the elemental tetrad of Pythagoras.

Now tell me, what man, by heaven, could wish to stick his head into the halter of marriage if, as your wise-acres have the habit of doing, he first weighed with himself the inconveniences of wedded life? Or what woman would ever admit her husband to her person, if she had heard or thought about the dangerous pains of child-birth and the irksomeness of bringing up a child? But since you owe your existence to the marriage-bed, and marriage is owing to Anoia, a servant of mine, you can see how vastly indebted you are to me! Then, too, would a woman who has gone through all this, wish to make a second venture, if the power and influence of my Lethe did not attend her? And in spite of what Lucretius claims, Venus herself would not deny that without the addition of my presence her strength would be enfeebled and in-effectual. So it is that from this brisk and silly little game of mine come forth the haughty philosophers (to whose places those who are vulgarly called monks have now succeeded), and kings in their scarlet, pious priests, and triply most holy popes; also, finally, that assembly of the gods of the poets, so numerous that Olympus, spacious as it is, can hardly accommodate the crowd.

[6] But let it be accounted a little thing that the seed-plot and source of existence are mine, if I do not show that whatever is profitable in any life is also of my giving. For what about it? Can life be called life at all if you take away pleasure? . . . You applaud! I knew that none of you is so wise—or rather so foolish—no, I prefer to say so wise—as to err on that point. Even the famous Stoics do not really scorn pleasure, but they studiously dissemble

and attack it in public with a thousand reproaches, only to the end that, with other people scared off, they may enjoy it more liberally. But let them tell me, by Jove, what part of life is not sad, unpleasant, graceless, flat, and burdensome, unless you have pleasure added to it, that is, a seasoning of folly? As proof of this, there is extant that lovely tribute to me by Sophocles, who can never be sufficiently praised, "To know nothing affords the happiest life"; and he would be authority enough, but come, I will open the whole matter, step by step.

First of all, who does not know that the earliest period of a man's life is by far the happiest for him and by far the most pleasant for all about him? What is it in children, that we should kiss them the way we do, and cuddle them, and fondle them—so that even an enemy would give aid to one of that age—except this enchantment of folly, which prudent nature carefully bestows on the newly born; so that by this pleasure, as a sort of prepayment, they win the favor of their nurses and parents and make these forget the pains of bringing them up. After this comes adolescence. How welcome it is in every home! How well everyone wishes it! How studiously does everyone promote it, how officiously they lend it the helping hand! But, I ask, whence comes this grace of youth? Whence but from me, by whose favor the young know so little—and how lightly worn is that little! And presently when lads grown larger begin, through experience and discipline, to have some smack of manhood, I am a liar if by the same token the brightness of their beauty does not fade, their quickness diminish, their wit lose its edge, their vigor slacken. The farther one gets from me, then, the less and less he lives, until *molesta senectus* (that is, irksome old age) arrives, hateful to others, to be sure, but also and more so to itself.

Old age would not be tolerable to any mortal at all, were it not that I, out of pity for its troubles, stand once more at its right hand; and just as the gods of the poets customarily save, by some metamorphosis or other, those who are dying, in like manner I bring those who have one foot in the grave back to their infancy again, for as long as possible; so that the folk are not far off in speaking of them as "in their second childhood." If anyone would like to know the method of bringing about this alteration, I shall not conceal it. I lead them to my spring of Lethe—for that stream rises in the Fortunate Isles, and only a little rivulet of it flows in the underworld—so that then and there they may drink draughts of forgetfulness. With their cares of mind purged away, by gentle stages they become young again. But now, you say, they merely dote, and play the fool. Yes, quite so. But precisely this it is to renew one's infancy. Is to be childish anything other than to dote and play the fool? As if in that age the greatest joy were not this, that one knows nothing! For who does not dread and shun as a prodigy the boy who has a man's wisdom? As the proverb current among the folk has it, "I hate a boy of premature wisdom." Who could bear to converse or transact business with an old man who should join to his long experience of things, an equal vigor of mind and sharpness of judgment? Hence it is that an old man dotes, thanks to me.

Yet this dotard of mind, meanwhile, is exempt from those carking cares by which your wise man is distracted. My dotard, too, is still an acceptable pot-companion. He does not feel life's tedium, which a younger constitution can scarce abide. Occasionally, like the old gentleman in Plautus, he goes back to conning those three letters, *a*, *m*, *o*—the unhappiest man in the world if he had his wits about him; but meanwhile happy, through my grace, a source of pleasure to his friends, a hail-fellow-well-met. Thus it is that, in Homer, speech sweeter than honey flows from the lips of Nestor, while that of Achilles is bitter; and in the same author the old men sitting on the wall utter gracious and elegant discourse. On this one score, indeed, the old even have an advantage over real childhood, which is sweet but tongue-tied, and lacks the chief solace of life, uninhibited garrulousness. Add to this that the old take great pleasure in children, and children in turn are delighted with the old. "God ever brings like to like." For wherein do they differ, except that age is more wrinkled and has counted more birthdays? Otherwise, their whitish hair, mouth without teeth, shortened body, appetite for milk, babbling, chatter, toying, shortness of memory, heedlessness, and all their other traits, agree exactly. And the farther the old proceed in age, the nearer they come back to the semblance of childhood; until like children indeed, having no weariness of life or sense of death, they take leave of the world.

Now let anyone that will compare this boon of mine with the metamorphoses produced by other gods. Those which they worked when angry it is not well to mention; but take the stories of people toward whom they were especially friendly. They would transform somebody into a tree, or a bird, or a cicada, or even into a snake; as if this were not to perish indeed—to be made into something else! But I restore the very same man to the best and happiest part of his life. And if mortals would abstain utterly from any contact with wisdom, and live out their span continuously in my company, there would not be any such thing as old age, but in happiness they would enjoy perpetual youth. For do you not see that the austere fellows who are buried in the study of philosophy, or condemned to difficult and wracking business, grow old even before they have been young—and this because by cares and continual hard driving of their brains they insensibly exhaust their spirits and dry up their radical moisture? On the contrary, my morons are as plump and sleek as the hogs of Acarnania (as the saying is), with complexions well cared for, never feeling the touch of old age; unless, as rarely happens, they catch something by contagion from the wise—so true is it that the life of man is not destined to be in every respect happy.

These arguments have the strong support of a proverb current among the folk; as they often say, "Folly is the one thing that makes fleeting youth linger and keeps ugly old age away." And rightly do they bruit it about concerning the people of Brabant, that although time brings prudence to others, the older Brabanters grow the more foolish they are. Yet no other race is more genial than theirs in the ordinary converse of life, and no other race feels so little the misery of old age. Neighbors to the Brabanters, by affinity of temperament as much as by geography, are my Hollanders—for why should I not call mine those who are such eager amateurs of folly that they have won a proverbial name for it, a name they are not ashamed of, but bandy back and forth among themselves?

Go, foolish mortals, and vainly seek for your Medeas and Circes and Venuses and Auroras, and the unknown fountain in which you may restore your youth! When all the time I alone have that power; I alone use it. In my shop is that miraculous juice with which the daughter of Memnon lengthened the days of her grandfather Tithonus. I am that Venus by whose favor Phaon grew young again so that he might be loved so much by Sappho. Mine are those herbs (if they exist), mine that fountain, mine the spells which not only bring back departed youth but, still better, preserve it in perpetuity. If, then, all of you subscribe to this sentiment, that nothing is better than adolescence or more undesirable than age, I think you must see how much you owe to me, who conserve so great a good and fend off so great an evil.

[7] But what am I doing, talking about mortal men? Survey the universal sky, and you may cast my name in my teeth if you can find anyone at all among the gods who is not foul and despicable except so far as he is graced by my divine power. For why is Bacchus always young and curly-haired? Simply because, frantic and giddy, he passes his life in feasts, routs, dances, and games, and has no tittle of converse with Pallas. So far is he from wanting to be accounted wise, in brief, that it tickles him to be worshipped in gambols and sport; nor is he offended by the proverb which gave him the nickname of fool, as thus: "More foolish than Morychus." For as time went on they changed his name to Morychus, because the wanton countryfolk used to smear his statue, placed before the gates of his temple, with new wine and fresh figs. And then what scoffs the Old Comedy throws at him! "O stupid god," they say, "and worthy to be born from a thigh!" But who would not choose to be stupid and foolish Bacchus, always festive, always downy of cheek, always

bringing gaiety and delight to all, rather than to be "deep-counselled" Jove, who frightens everybody, or Pan in his peevishness, infecting all things with his disorders, or Vulcan, full of cinders and foul from the labors of his shop, or even Pallas herself, "always peering grimly," with her Gorgon's head and fearful spear? Why is Cupid forever a boy? Why, but because he is a trifler, and cannot do or even consider anything at all sane. Why does the beauty of the aureate Venus keep an eternal spring? Surely because she is related to me; whence also she bears in her face my father's color, and for that reason in Homer she is "golden Aphrodite." Lastly, she laughs perpetually, if we can in anything believe the poets or their rivals, the sculptors. What divinity did the Romans ever worship more devoutly than Flora, that breeder of all delights? Nay, if one faithfully seeks in Homer to learn the story of the austere gods, he will find it replete with folly. But why stop to record the doings of the others, when you know so well the loves and pastimes of Jove the Thunderer himself? When the chaste Diana, forgetting her sex, does nothing but hunt, being all the time desperately in love with Endymion?

But yet I should prefer that they heard their exploits recited by Momus, from whom they used to hear them often; till lately they became wroth and cast him head first, along with Ate, down to earth, just because he was petulant and interrupted, with his wisdom, the felicity of the gods. Nor do any mortals consider the exile worthy of hospitality, especially since there is no place for him in the courts of princes, where my Kolakia holds top place; Momus could no more get along with her than a wolf with a lamb. With that fellow thus disposed of, the gods now play the fool much more freely and pleasantly, "doing all things carelessly," as father Homer puts it; that is to say, without a censor. For what merry pranks will not the ramshackle god, Priapus, afford? What games will not Mercury play, with his thefts and deceits? And is it not the custom for Vulcan to act as jester at the banquets of the gods, and partly by his lameness, partly by his taunts, partly by his silly sayings, to enliven the community drinking? Then there is also that old amorist, Silenus, who is wont to dance the cancan, together with Polyphemus and his lyre-twanging, and the nymphs with their barefoot ballet. The half-goat satyrs act out interludes. Stupid Pan moves the laughter of all by some ballad, which the gods prefer above hearing the Muses themselves, especially when they begin to be drenched with nectar. And why go on to rehearse what the drunken gods so fitly do after the banquet? Such foolish things, so help me, that sometimes I, though I am Folly, cannot keep from laughing. Yet it is better at this point to think of Harpocrates, for fear some spy among the gods may overhear us telling those things which Momus did not tell with impunity.

[8] But now the time has come when, following the pattern of Homer, we should turn our backs on the heavens and travel down again to earth, where likewise we shall perceive nothing joyous or fortunate except by my favor. First of all, you see with what foresight nature, the source and artificer of the human race, has made provision that this race shall never lack its seasoning of folly. For since, by the Stoic definitions, wisdom is no other than to be governed by reason, while folly is to be moved at the whim of the passions, Jupiter, to the end, obviously, that

the life of mankind should not be sad and harsh, put in—how much more of passions than of reason? Well, the proportions run about one pound to half an ounce. Besides, he imprisoned reason in a cramped corner of the head, and turned over all the rest of the body to the emotions. After that he instated two most violent tyrants, as it were, in opposition to reason: anger, which holds the citadel of the breast, and consequently the very spring of life, the heart; and lust, which rules a broad empire lower down, even to the privy parts. How much reason is good for, against these twin forces, the ordinary life of men sufficiently reveals when reason—and it is all she can do—shouts out her prohibitions until she is hoarse and dictates formulas of virtue. But the passions simply bid their so-called king go hang himself, and more brazenly roar down the opposition, until the man, tired out as well, willingly yields and knuckles under.

But a tiny bit more than a grain of reason is vouchsafed to the male, born as he is for handling affairs; and in order that he might give and take counsel in manly fashion, he brought me into the council chamber, as everywhere else. Right off I gave him advice worthy of myself: namely, that he should form an alliance with woman—a stupid animal, God wot, and a giddy one, yet funny and sweet—so that in domestic familiarity her folly might leaven the lumpishness of the male temperament. When Plato shows himself in doubt whether to place woman in the class of rational creatures or in that of brutes, he only wishes to point out how flagrant is the folly of the sex. For if by chance some woman wishes to be thought of as wise, she does nothing but show herself twice a fool. It is as if one took a bull to the masseuse, a thing quite "against the grain," as the phrase is. It is doubly a fault, you know, when against nature one assumes the color of a virtue, warping one's character in a direction not its own. Just as, according to the proverb of the Greeks, "an ape is always an ape, though dressed in scarlet," so a woman is always a woman—that is, a fool—whatever part she may have chosen to play.

And yet I do not suppose the female sex is so foolish as to become incensed at me for this, that I, a woman and Folly as well, attribute folly to women. For if they rightly consider the matter, they are bound to score up a credit to Folly for this, that in many respects they are better off than men. For one thing, they have the gift of beauty, which with good reason they prefer above all things else. Assisted by it, they wield a tyranny over tyrants themselves. Whence but from the malady of prudence comes that horrendous visage, rough as to skin, with an undergrowth of beard and a suggestion of senility, in men? Whereas the cheeks of women are always bare and smooth, their voice gentle, their skin soft, as if presenting a picture of perpetual youth. Furthermore, what else do they want in life but to be as attractive as possible to men? Do not all their trimmings and cosmetics have this end in view, and all their baths, fittings, creams, scents, as well—and all those arts of making up, painting, and fashioning the face, eyes, and skin? Just so. And by what other sponsor are they better recommended to men than by folly? What is there that men will not permit to women? But for what consideration, except pleasure? And women please by no other thing than their folly. The truth of this no one will deny who has considered what nonsense a man talks with a woman, and what quaint tricks he plays, as often as he has a mind to enjoy the delights of feminine society.

You have heard, then, about the source whence flows the first and sovereign solace of life. But there are some men, principally old ones, who are topers rather than womanizers, and decree that the highest pleasure lies in bouts of drinking. Whether there can be any genteel entertainment with no woman present, let others decide. This remains certain: without some relish of folly, no banquet is pleasing. Hence if someone is not present who creates laughter by his real or simulated folly, the revellers send out and get a comedian for hire, or bring in some other silly parasite, who by his jests—that is, foolish gibes—will drive silence and moroseness away from the company. For what avails it to load the belly with all those fine wines, savory dishes, and rare meats, if similarly our eyes and ears, our whole souls, do not batten on laughter, jests, and witticisms? I am the only confectioner of these desserts. Yes, and those other ceremonies of banquets, such as choosing a king by lot, playing at dice, drinking healths, sending the cups around, singing in rounds and relays, dancing, mimicking—the Seven Sages of Greece did not discover these for the solace of mankind; I did. The nature of all this sort of thing is such that the more of folly it has in it, the more it advantages the life of men, which surely ought not to be called life at all if it is unhappy. Yet unhappy it must needs be, unless by diversions of this kind you chase away ennui, the brother of unhappiness.

[9] Yet there are others, perhaps, who do not care for this department of pleasure either, but find satisfaction in the love and familiar society of friends, letting it be known

that friendship uniquely deserves to be preferred above all
else; as being so necessary a thing that not air, fire, or
water is more so; and so delightful that he who would
take it from the world would take the sun from the sky;
and lastly so honorable (as if honor had something to do
with the subject) that the philosophers themselves have
not hesitated to name it among the greatest goods. But
what if I demonstrate that I am both the stem and the
stern of this admired good also? And I shall not demonstrate it by ambiguous syllogisms, sorites, horned dilem-
mas, or any other sophistical subtleties of that sort; but by
crude common sense, as the phrase is, I shall point it out
as plainly as if with my finger. Go to! Conniving at your
friends' vices, passing them over, being blind to them and
deceived by them, even loving and admiring your friends'
egregious faults as if they were virtues—does not this
seem pretty close to folly? Think a moment of the fellow
who kisses the mole on his mistress's neck, or of the other
who is delighted by the growth on his little lady's nose, or
of the father who says of his cross-eyed son that his eyes
twinkle? What is all this, I ask you, but sheer folly? Ay,
you all vote—triple and quadruple foolishness! Yet this
same foolishness both joins friends and, after joining them,
keeps their friendship alive.

I am talking about mortal men, of whom none is born
without faults; that one is best who is afflicted with the
fewest of them. Among the god-like Stoics, of course,
either friendship does not spring up at all, or there exists a
certain austere and cold variety of it, and even this in but
few cases—I have scruples against saying, in none. For
the greater number of mankind play the fool; nay, there
is no one who does not dote in many ways; and close

friendship grows up only between equals. Grant that a certain mutual benevolence may exist among these severe thinkers, it is by no means steady or enduring—that is, among men who are morose and equipped with such eyesight that they scan the faults of their friends with the keen vision of an eagle or of an Epidaurian serpent, though they are sand-blind toward their own vices, not seeing the pack that hangs behind their own backs. Since, then, the nature of man is such that one can discover no constitution which is not liable to great faults—and add to this all the great diversity of ages and of education, all the slips, all the mistakes, all the accidents, of mortal life —how can the pleasure of friendship subsist for an hour between those Arguses, unless it is attended by that which the Greeks so aptly call εὐήθεια, which you may translate either as "folly" or as "easy-going ways." But what? Is not Cupid, that well-known author and parent of all deep affection, stricken right in the eyes, so that with him "what is not beautiful seems so"? In like manner, it comes to pass among you that what each desires seems fair to each; "the gaffer dotes on the gammer, and the knave on the wench." These things go on everywhere, and are laughed at, but, ridiculous as they are, they cement and bind together our agreeable social life.

What has been said of friendship applies even better to marriage, which is an indivisible bond of life. Good Lord, what divorces, or worse things, would not happen all over the place, were not the domestic association of man and woman propped up and fostered by flattery, by jesting, by pliableness, ignorance, dissimulation—satellites of mine, remember! Mercy me, how few marriages would come off, if the husband prudently inquired what tricks his seemingly coy and modest little lady had played long before the wedding! And still fewer, though entered upon, would last, did not most of the wife's doings escape her husband's knowledge, through his negligence or stupidity. But these blessings are owed to Folly. She brings it about that the wife pleases the husband, the husband pleases the wife, the household is tranquil, the alliance holds. A husband is laughed at, called cuckoo, cuckold, or what not, when he kisses away the tears of his whorish wife; but how much happier thus to be deceived than to harass himself by an unresting jealousy and to spoil everything with distressing brawls.

In sum, no society, no union in life, could be either pleasant or lasting without me. A people does not for long tolerate its prince, or a master tolerate his servant, a handmaiden her mistress, a teacher his student, a friend his friend, a wife her husband, a landlord his tenant, a partner his partner, or a boarder his fellow-boarder, except as they mutually or by turns are mistaken, on occasion flatter, on occasion wisely wink, and otherwise soothe themselves with the sweetness of folly.

[10] Now I am aware that this seems the most that can be said, but you are going to hear what is greater. I ask you: will he who hates himself love anyone? Will he who does not get along with himself agree with another? Or will he who is disagreeable and irksome to himself bring pleasure to any? No one would say so, unless he were himself more foolish than Folly. But were you to bar me out, each man would be so incapable of getting along with any other that he would become a stench in his own nostrils, his possessions would be filthy rags, and he would be hateful to himself. The reason for this is that nature, in

many respects a stepmother rather than a mother, has sowed some seed of evil in the breasts of mortal men, and particularly of men somewhat judicious, which makes them dissatisfied with what is their own, while admiring what belongs to another. Thus it comes about that every endowment, every grace and elegance of life, suffers taint and is lost. For what avails beauty, chiefest gift of the immortal gods, if it is touched by the malady of decay? What price youth, if it is infected by the germs of age? And finally, what in the whole business of life, whether private or public, can you carry through with grace—for not only in art but in every action the great thing is to do whatever you do in a seemly way—except as this lady, Philautia, stands at your right hand, she who by merit takes the place of sister to me, and everywhere plays my part with fidelity?

For what is so foolish as to be satisfied with yourself? Or to admire yourself? Yet on the other hand, if you are displeased with yourself, what can you do that is pleasing or graceful or seemly? Take this ingredient from life, and at once the orator, like his style, will be flat and cold, the musician will be as sour as his notes, the actor, with all his mimicry, will be hissed from the stage, the painter as well as his pictures will be cheap, and the poor doctor will famish among his poor medicines. Without self-love, though you may be a handsome Nireus, you will appear like Thersites; you will seem a Nestor, though a Phaon; a sow instead of Minerva, tongue-tied instead of eloquent, a gawk instead of a man of the world. That is how necessary it is to capture your own fancy, and to appreciate your own value by a bit of self-applause, before you can be held in price by others. Finally, since the better part of happiness is to wish to be what you are, why certainly my Philautia reaches that end by a short cut; so that no one is ashamed of his own looks, no one regrets his own temperament, or feels shame for his race, his locality, his profession, or his fatherland. An Irishman does not want to change places with an Italian, or a Thracian with an Athenian, or a Scythian with a dweller in the Fortunate Isles. Oh, the singular foresight of nature, who, in spite of such differences of condition, equalizes all things! Where she has withheld some of her bounties, there she is wont to add a little more self-love; but I have made a foolish saying, for self-love is itself the greatest bounty of nature.

[11] May I not affirm, indeed, that you will find no great exploit undertaken, no important arts invented, except at my prompting? As, for instance, is not war the seed-plot and fountain of renowned actions? Yet what is more foolish than to enter upon a conflict for I know not what causes, wherein each side reaps more of loss than of gain? As for those who fall, as was said of the Megarians, "no particulars." And when armored ranks engage each other and bugles bray with harsh accord, of what use are those wise men, who, exhausted by studies, scarce maintain any life in their thin, cold blood? The day belongs to stout, gross fellows; the littler wit they have, the bolder they are—unless, forsooth, you prefer a soldier like Demosthenes, who, since he agreed with the poetic sentiment of Archilochus, dropped his shield and ran, as cowardly in warfare as he was consummate in eloquence. But wise planning, they say, is of most importance in war. Yes, on the part of a general, I grant; yet is it military, not philosophical, wisdom. Far otherwise: this famous game of war is played by parasites, panders,

bandits, assassins, peasants, sots, bankrupts, and such other dregs of mankind; never by philosophers, with their candles of wisdom.

How ineffective these philosophers are for the work of real life, the one and only Socrates himself, who was judged wisest by (not the wisest) oracle of Apollo, will serve for proof. When he tried to urge something, I know not what, in public, he hastily withdrew to the accompaniment of loud laughter from all quarters. Yet Socrates was not altogether foolish in this one respect, that he repudiated the epithet "wise," and gave it over to God; he also cherished the opinion that a wise man should abstain from meddling in the public business of the commonwealth. To be sure, he ought rather to have admonished us that one who wishes to have a place in the ranks of men should abstain from wisdom itself. And then, what but his wisdom drove him, once he had been impeached, to drink the hemlock? For while he disputed and reasoned of clouds and ideas, while he measured the feet of a flea, and marvelled at the voice of a gnat, he did not fathom the commonest concerns of life. But with this teacher standing in peril of death, comes now his scholar Plato, that remarkable (shall we say?) advocate, who was so abashed by the murmur of the audience that he could scarcely deliver the well-known half of his first sentence. And what shall I say of Theophrastus? When he was starting to make a speech, he was suddenly struck dumb, as if he had caught sight of a wolf. Could he have heartened a soldier going into battle? Thanks to the timorousness of his nature, Isocrates never dared open his mouth in public. Marcus Tullius Cicero, father of Roman eloquence, used always to begin to speak with an unseemly kind of trembling, like a boy out of breath and gasping; and Quintilian interprets this as revealing the wise orator, conscious of the difficulty of his task. But when he so writes, does he not plainly confess that wisdom is but an obstacle to speaking eloquently? What would they do if the case were to be argued with cold steel, when they are bloodless with fear in a contest of mere words?

But in God's good grace, after everything else, that famous saying of Plato's is trotted out: "Happy is the state where philosophers are made kings, or whose kings become philosophers!" No, if you consult the historians, you will find, as plain as day, that nowhere have princes been so baneful to commonwealths as where the rule has devolved upon some philosophaster or bookish fellow. The Catos, I suggest, give support enough to this point: one of them was always vexing the tranquility of the republic by hare-brained accusations, and the other totally destroyed the liberty of the Roman people, defending it, all the while, as wisely as you please. But to the Catos add your Brutus, your Cassius, the Gracchi, and even Cicero himself, who was no less fatal to the commonwealth of Rome than Demosthenes was to Athens. Then there is Marcus Aurelius—so that we may allow there was once a good emperor, I have just now been able to dig him up —who was vexatious and even hateful to the citizens for the very reason that he was so good a philosopher. I say that we must allow he was a good emperor, yet by leaving behind such a son as his, he certainly harmed the state more than he had benefited it by his good management. For a fact, this whole species of men who give themselves over to the pursuit of wisdom run to unluckiness in most things, and in none so much as in the children they beget;

nature ordering it thus, I suggest, that the mischief of wisdom shall not be too generally insinuated into the race. Thus, as we all know, Cicero had a son quite unlike his ancestors, and the wise Socrates had children who "favored the mother somewhat more than the father," as one author rather nicely put it; that is, they were fools.

If it were merely that your wise men approach public affairs precisely "as asses do a lyre," it might be borne; but they are no more dexterous in performing any of life's duties. Take your sage to a feast, and he will mar the good cheer either by a morose silence or by conducting a quiz. Invite him to a ball, and you learn how a camel dances. If you carry him to a play, he will dampen the mirth of the audience, and, a modern Cato, he will be forced to walk out of the theater because he cannot put off his gravity. If he engages in conversation, on a sudden it is a case of the wolf in the story. If something is to be bought, or a contract made, if, in short, any of those things without which our daily life could not be carried on must be done, you will say that this wiseacre is no man, but dead wood. Thus he can be of little use to himself, his country, or his family, and all because he is inexpert in everyday matters, and far out of step with general ways of thinking and modes of life among the folk; by the same token he is bound to fall into odium, through the great diversity between his and their lives and minds. For what that passes among mortals everywhere is not full of folly, done by fools in the presence of fools? If some one wishes to set up an opposition to the whole business, I should urge him to imitate Timon and move to some wilderness, where he may enjoy his wisdom alone.

[12] But let me get back to what I had outlined. What power was it drew together into civil society those stony, wooden, and wild people, if not flattery? That famed lyre of Amphion and that other of Orpheus mean nothing else than this. When the Roman people were hatching revolutions, what recalled them to civic concord? A philosophical oration, perhaps? No, not that. It was a silly and puerile story made up about the belly and the other members of the body. The tale Themistocles told about a fox and a hedge-hog worked in the same way. What oration by a wise man could have availed so well as did the fictitious white hind of Sertorius, or as the silly object-lesson of the Spartan about the two puppies, or the other one about pulling the hair out of horses' tails? I am saying nothing of Minos and Numa, both of whom ruled the foolish multitude by making up fables; for by such toys that great and powerful beast, the people, is to be controlled. Again, what city ever adopted the doctrines of Socrates or the laws framed by Plato or Aristotle? On the other hand, what persuaded the three Decii to give themselves, for their country's sake, to the gods of the underworld? What carried Quintus Curtius into that fissure, if not mere glory —a certain exceedingly lovely siren who, strangely enough, is frowned upon by your wise men. For, as they point out, what is more foolish than for a candidate seeking office to flatter the people, to buy their favor with doles, to court the applause of so many fools, to be pleased by their shouts, to be carried about in parades as if he were a spectacle for the populace, to have his statue in the marketplace? To all these add the adoption of new names, and nicknames; then add those divine honors paid to very sorry fellows, and the deification, at great public cere-

monies, of criminal tyrants. This sort of thing is most arrant folly. One Democritus cannot suffice for laughing at it. Who denies this? And yet from this source arise all those memorable exploits of doughty heroes which are extolled by the pens of so many eloquent men. The same foolishness gave rise to cities, by it empires are maintained, along with magistracy, religion, policy, and courts; nor is human life in general anything but a kind of fool's game.

Let me say a word about the arts. What but a thirst for glory has enlisted the talents of men in the task of inventing and transmitting to posterity all these learned disciplines, which they deem so wonderful? Men who really are among the most foolish have thought that by nights without sleep, and by their sweat, they could purchase fame—I know not what sort of fame, but certainly nothing could be more empty. Yet at any rate you owe these choice blessings of life to Folly, and—what is the cream of the jest—you reap the fruits of a madness you need not share.

[13] And now, since I have made good my title to renown for courage and resourcefulness, suppose I should lay claim also to prudence? "But," someone will say, "with no more effort you might mix fire and water." Perhaps so. Still, I shall have good success in this, I am convinced, if only you will lend me, as you have done so far, your ears and minds. And first, if prudence depends upon experience of affairs, to whom does the honor of this attribute belong? To the wise man, who, by reason partly of modesty and partly of faint-heartedness, will attempt no action? Or to the fool, who is not deterred from any enterprise by modesty, of which he is innocent, or by

peril, which he never pauses to weigh? The wise man runs to books of the ancients and learns from them a merely verbal shrewdness. The fool arrives at true prudence, if I am not deceived, by addressing himself at once to the business and taking his chances. Homer seems to have seen this, for all that he was blind, when he said, "Even a fool is wise after a thing is done." There are two great obstacles to developing a knowledge of affairs—shame, which throws a smoke over the understanding, and fear, which, once danger has been sighted, dissuades from going through with an exploit. Folly, with a grand gesture, frees us from both. Never to feel shame, to dare anything —few mortals know to what further blessings these will carry us!

Yet if they prefer to have that prudence which consists in the mere discernment of things, then hear, I adjure you, how far they are from it who still vaunt themselves upon the name. For first of all, the fact is that all human affairs, like the Sileni of Alcibiades, have two aspects, each quite different from the other; even to the point that what at first blush (as the phrase goes) seems to be death may prove, if you look further into it, to be life. What at first sight is beautiful may really be ugly; the apparently wealthy may be poorest of all; the disgraceful, glorious; the learned, ignorant; the robust, feeble; the noble, base; the joyous, sad; the favorable, adverse; what is friendly, an enemy; and what is wholesome, poisonous. In brief, you find all things suddenly reversed, when you open up the Silenus. Perhaps this seems too philosophical a saying; but come, with the help of a somewhat fat Minerva (to use an old expression), I shall make it more clear. Who would not avow that the king is a rich and great lord?

Yet let the king be unfurnished in goods of the spirit, let him find satisfaction in nothing, and you see in a trice that he is the poorest of men. Suppose that his soul is given over to vices; now he is a vile slave. In like manner one might philosophize concerning others also, but let this one serve as an example.

But where, one asks, does it all lead? Have patience, and let us carry it further. If a person were to try stripping the disguises from actors while they play a scene upon the stage, showing to the audience their real looks and the faces they were born with, would not such a one spoil the whole play? And would not the spectators think he deserved to be driven out of the theater with brickbats, as a drunken disturber? For at once a new order of things would be apparent. The actor who played a woman would now be seen a man; he who a moment ago appeared young, is old; he who but now was a king, is suddenly an hostler; and he who played the god is a sorry little scrub. Destroy the illusion and any play is ruined. It is the paint and trappings that take the eyes of spectators. Now what else is the whole life of mortals but a sort of comedy, in which the various actors, disguised by various costumes and masks, walk on and play each one his part, until the manager waves them off the stage? Moreover, this manager frequently bids the same actor go back in a different costume, so that he who has but lately played the king in scarlet now acts the flunkey in patched clothes. Thus all things are presented by shadows; yet this play is put on in no other way.

But suppose, right here, some wise man who has dropped down from the sky should suddenly confront me and cry out that the person whom the world has accepted as a god and a master is not even a man, because he is driven sheeplike by his passions; that he is the lowest slave, because he willingly serves so many and such base masters. Or again, suppose the visitor should command some one mourning his father's death to laugh, because now his father has really begun to live—for in a sense our earthly life is but a kind of death. Suppose him to address another who is glorying in his ancestry, and to call him low and base-born because he is so far from virtue, the only true fount of nobility. Suppose him to speak of others in like vein. I ask you, what would he get by it, except to be considered by everyone as insane and raving? As nothing is more foolish than wisdom out of place, so nothing is more imprudent than unseasonable prudence. And he is unseasonable who does not accommodate himself to things as they are, who is "unwilling to follow the market," who does not keep in mind at least that rule of conviviality, "Either drink or get out"; who demands, in short, that the play should no longer be a play. The part of a truly prudent man, on the contrary, is (since we are mortal) not to aspire to wisdom beyond his station, and either, along with the rest of the crowd, pretend not to notice anything, or affably and companionably be deceived. But that, they tell us, is folly. Indeed, I shall not deny it; only let them, on their side, allow that it is also to play out the comedy of life.

[14] As for the next, O ye immortal gods! Shall I speak or be silent? But why should I be silent, when it is more true than truth? Yet haply for such an undertaking it might be well to send up to Helicon and fetch the Muses, whom the poets are wont to invoke, quite often on most trivial occasions. Therefore, be present for a brief

season, daughters of Jove, while I show to the world that one never attains to that renowned wisdom, which the wise themselves call the citadel of happiness, except by taking Folly as guide. And first, it is beyond dispute that all emotions belong to folly. Indeed, we distinguish a wise man from a fool by this, that reason governs the one, and passion the other. Thus the Stoics take away from the wise man all perturbations of the soul, as so many diseases. Yet these passions not only discharge the office of mentor and guide to such as are pressing toward the gate of wisdom, but they also assist in every exercise of virtue as spurs and goads—persuaders, as it were—to well doing. Although that double-strength Stoic, Seneca, stoutly denies this, subtracting from the wise man any and every emotion, yet in doing so he leaves him no man at all but rather a new kind of god, or demiurgos, who never existed and will never emerge. Nay, to speak more plainly, he creates a marble simulacrum of a man, a senseless block, completely alien to every human feeling.

Well, if they want it so, I give them joy of this wise man of theirs. They may love him with no fear of a rival, and may live with him in Plato's republic, or, if they prefer, in the world of ideas, or in the gardens of Tantalus. For who would not startle at such a man, as at an apparition or ghost, and shun him? He would be insensible to any natural sympathy, no more moved by feelings of love or pity than as if he were solid flint or Marpesian stone. Nothing gets by him; he never makes a mistake; as if another Lynceus, there is no thing he does not see; he measures everything with a standard rule; he forgives nothing; he alone is satisfied with himself alone, uniquely rich, uniquely sane, uniquely a king, uniquely a free man;

in short, uniquely all things, but notably unique in his own judgment; he values no friend, himself the friend of none; he does not hesitate to bid the gods go hang themselves; he condemns as unwholesome whatever life may offer, and derides it. An animal of that description is your perfect wise man. I ask you, if it were a matter of votes, what city would choose such a one as magistrate? What army would want that kind of general? Nay, what woman would pick, or put up with, that kind of husband? What host would have such a guest? Who would not prefer just anyone from the middle ranks of human foolhood, who, being a fool, would be better prepared either to command fools or to obey them; who would please those like himself, that is, nearly everyone; who would be kind to his wife, welcome to his friends, a boon companion, an acceptable dinner-guest; and lastly, who would consider nothing human to be alien to him. But I grew bored with that wise man some time ago; let the speech betake itself to advantages not yet touched upon.

[15] Come, then, and suppose a man could look from a high tower, as the poets say Jove is in the habit of doing. To how many calamities would he see the life of man subject! How painful, how messy, man's birth! How irksome his rearing—his childhood exposed to so many hurts, his youth beset by so many problems! Then age is a burden; the certainty of death is inexorable. Diseases infest life's every way; accidents threaten, troubles assail without warning; there is nothing that is not tainted with gall. Nor can I recite all those evils which man suffers at the hands of man; poverty is in this class, and imprisonment, infamy, shame, tortures, snares, treachery, slander, litigation, fraud. But you see I am engaged in "counting the

sand." For what offenses men have deserved these things, or what angry god compelled them to be born to such miseries, it is no business of mine to discuss at the moment. But if one ponders upon the evils I speak of, will not one approve the example, pitiable as it is, set by the Milesian virgins? And yet who are the people that, merely because of weariness of life, have hastened their fate? Were they not the people who lived next door to wisdom? Among them, to pass over such as Diogenes, Xenocrates, Cato, Cassius, and Brutus, there was even Chiron, who, though he had the privilege of being immortal, took the option of death. You will observe, I am sure, what would happen if men generally became wise: there would be need for some fresh clay and for another potter like Prometheus.

But aided in part by ignorance, and in part by inadvertence, sometimes by forgetfulness of evil, sometimes by hope of good, sprinkling in a few honeyed delights at certain seasons, I bring relief from these ills; so that men are unwilling to relinquish their lives even when, by the exactly measured thread of the Fates, life is due to relinquish them. The less reason they have for remaining alive, the more they seem to delight in living—so far are they from being stricken with any tedium of life. Surely it is because of my bounty that you everywhere see these old fellows of Nestor's age, with hardly the shape of a man left them, babbling and silly, toothless, white-haired, bald—or better, let me describe them in the words of Aristophanes, "slovenly, crooked, wrinkled, glabrous, toothless, and toolless." And yet you see them still enjoying life so much and trying to be young so hard that one of them dyes his white hair, another covers his baldness with a wig, another enjoys the use of borrowed teeth, probably taken from the jaw of a pig; another is perishing miserably for love of some girl, and outdoes any adolescent in his amorous absurdities. And for one of these old candidates for the tomb, mere bent sticks as they are, to marry with a plump young wife—without dowry, to be sure, and destined for the pleasure of others—has become so common that it will soon be the approved thing. But the best sport of all is to watch our old women, already moribund with age, so cadaverous that you would think they had come back from their graves, having always on their tongues the phrase, "It's good to be alive!" and always in heat besides; as the Greeks put it, they "play the goat," having at hand some Phaon, engaged at a high fee. They industriously smear their faces with paint, never getting away from a mirror; they pluck out hairs from the strangest places; they display their withered and foul breasts; with a quavering love-song they keep awake a tired desire; they tipple, and mingle with the groups of young women; they write love-letters. These capers are laughed at by everyone, with good reason, as being the silliest in the world. Yet the old ladies are satisfied with themselves, and in the meantime they swim in pleasure and anoint themselves all over with honey; they are happy, in a word, by courtesy of me. And as for the people who find it all too ridiculous, I want them to mull over the question whether it is not better to lead this sort of honeyed life in folly than to look for a rafter, as the phrase goes, suitable for a hanging. Besides, it makes no difference to my fools that such things may be held disgraceful by the crowd, since fools do not feel disgrace, or, if they feel it, they can easily pass it off. If a rock falls on your head, that is bad; but shame, infamy, opprobrium, and curses hurt only so far as they are felt. If one has no sense of them, they are not evils at all. What harm is it if everybody hisses you, so long as you applaud yourself? But to this happy end, only Folly avails.

[16] And now I seem to hear the philosophers disagreeing with me. But the true unhappiness, they say, is to be engrossed in folly, to err, to be deceived, not to know. Nay, this is to live as a man. Why they call it "unhappy" I cannot see. It is simply that men are born thus, trained thus, constituted thus; it is the common lot of all. Nothing can be called unhappy if it fulfils its own nature, unless you would conclude that a man ought to be pitied because he cannot fly about with the birds, and cannot run on four feet like the whole family of beasts, and is not armed with horns like a bull. But by the same token one will call the finest horse miserable because he has not learned grammar and does not eat cheese-cakes; one will call the bull unhappy because he is such a sorry wrestler. Hence, just as a horse ignorant of grammar is not miserable, a man who is a fool is not unhappy; the reason being that in each case the attribute is consistent with the nature.

But our logic-choppers have something else to urge. Knowledge of the sciences, they say, is peculiarly the attribute of man; using them as tools, he makes up in his powers for what nature withheld from him. As if this had the least semblance of truth—that nature, which expended so much exact care upon gnats, and upon herbs and flowers, should have fallen asleep over the making of man! So that he has need of sciences—which Theuth, that evil genius of the human race, excogitated for the hurt of man, and which are so far from furthering his hap-

piness that they actually hinder it. To that end they were
discovered, according to report, just as that wise king in
Plato wittily proves with respect to the invention of
letters. Thus the sciences crept in by stealth, along with
other banes of human life, and from the very sources
whence all evils flow—devils, let us say. Even the name
you call them shows this, for "daemons" means "those
who know" [δαήμονας = *scientes*].

The simple folk of the golden age flourished without
any armament of sciences, being guided only by nature and
instinct. For what need was there of grammar when all
spoke the same language, and had no other aim in speaking but that some one else should understand? What use
for dialectic, where there was no battle of opinions ranged
in contradiction to each other? What room for rhetoric,
when no man cared to make trouble for his neighbor?
Wherein was the study of law called for, when folk had
not learned the evil ways from which, we must admit, our
good laws arose. Then, moreover, they had too much
piety to search out, with a profane curiosity, the secrets
of nature; to investigate the dimensions, motions, and
influences of the stars, or the hidden causes of things;
deeming it a sacrilege for mortal man to try to know more
than is proper to his station. This madness of inquiring
what may lie beyond the sky never entered their heads.
But as the pristine simplicity of the golden age little by
little slipped away, first the arts were discovered—by
evil spirits, as I have told; but they were few in number
and accepted by few people. Later on, the superstition
of the Chaldeans and the frivolous curiosity of the Greeks
added hundreds of them—mere vexations of the spirit,

seeing that a single system of grammar will amply provide continuous torture through a long lifetime.

And yet among these disciplines the ones that approach nearest to common sense, that is, to folly, are held in highest esteem. Theologians are starved, naturalists find cold comfort, astrologers are mocked, and logicians are slighted. "The doctor alone is worth all the rest put together." Within the profession of medicine, furthermore, so far as any member is eminently unlearned, impudent, or careless, he is valued the more, even in the chambers of belted earls. For medicine, especially as now practised by many, is but a sub-division of the art of flattery, no less truly than is rhetoric. Lawyers have the next place after doctors, and I do not know but that they should have first place; with great unanimity the philosophers—not that I would say such a thing myself—are wont to ridicule the law as an ass. Yet great matters and little matters alike are settled by the arbitrament of these asses. They gather goodly freeholds with broad acres, while the theologian, after poring over chestfuls of the great corpus of divinity, gnaws on bitter beans, at the same time manfully waging war against lice and fleas. As those arts are more successful which have the greatest affinity with folly, so those people are by far the happiest who enjoy the privilege of avoiding all contact with the learned disciplines, and who follow nature as their only guide, since she is in no respect wanting, except as a mortal wishes to transgress the limits set for his status. Nature hates counterfeits; and that which is innocent of art gets along far the more prosperously.

Consider: among the several kinds of living creatures, do you not observe that the ones which live most happily are those which are farthest from any discipline, and which are controlled by no other master than nature? What could be more happy than the bees—or more wonderful? They do not seem to have all of the bodily senses; yet what has architecture discovered that can match their principles of construction? What philosopher has ever framed a republic equal to theirs? The horse, on the other hand, so far as he has senses like to man's, and travels about with companies of men, is also a partaker in human misfortunes. Thus many a horse actually feels shame to be outrun, and for that reason he becomes wind-broken by often racing. Or if the horse courts triumph in the wars, he is stuck through, and "bites the dust" along with his rider. I need not mention the cruel bits and sharpened spurs, the prison of a stable, the whips, batons, and tie-straps, the rider—in brief, all that tragedy of serf-dom to which he exposes himself when he imitates brave men and too zealously endeavors to wreak vengeance upon the enemy. How much more desirable, except for the traps laid by men, the life of flies and birds, living for the moment and solely by the light of nature! And if it happens that birds are shut up in cages and practise making the sounds of human speech, it is marvellous how they decline from their natural beauty and gaiety. At every level of life, what nature has ordained is more happy than what is adulterated by art.

Therefore I shall never praise enough that cock, who was really Pythagoras: though but one, he had been all things—a philosopher, a man, a woman, a king, a subject, a fish, a horse, a frog, I think even a sponge—and he came to the conclusion that no creature is more miserable than man; for all the others are satisfied with their natural limitations, but man alone strives to go beyond the bounds proper to his station. And among men, in turn, this cock ranked simpletons, on many counts, above the learned and great. That fellow Gryllus was not a little wiser than "Odysseus of the many counsels," when he elected to grunt in a sty rather than to expose himself, along with that worthy, to painful mishaps. It seems to me that Homer, the father of nonsense, does not disagree with these sentiments; he more than once applies to all mortals the epithets of "wretched and calamity-stricken," and still oftener he calls Ulysses, that pattern of wisdom, "miserable": whereas he never speaks so of Paris, or Ajax, or Achilles. Why should Ulysses be miserable, except that the wily and resourceful rogue never undertook anything without the advice of Pallas? He was overly wise, and got too far away from the guidance of nature. Hence it appears that among mortals they who are zealous for wisdom are farthest from happiness, being by the same token fools twice over: that is, although they are born men, they then so far forget their own station as to hanker after the life of the immortal gods; and on the example of the Giants, with arts and sciences as their engines they wage war on nature. So also those appear to be least unhappy who approach nearest to the temperament and simplicity of the beasts, nor ever undertake what is beyond man.

[17] Come, let us not test this with Stoic enthymemes, when we can demonstrate it by a single plain example. By the gods above, is there anything that is better off than that class of men whom we generally call morons, fools, halfwits, and zanies—the most beautiful names I know of! You see, I am telling you what at first blush may seem silly and absurd but is true many times over. For first of

all, these folk are free from all fear of death—and this fear, by Jove, is no piddling evil! They are free from tortures of conscience. They are not frightened by tales of ghosts, or scared to death by specters and goblins. They are not tormented by dread of impending evils, and they are not blown up with hope of future good. In short, they are not vexed by the thousand cares to which this life is subject. They do not feel shame or fear, they are not ambitious, they do not envy, they do not love. And finally, if they should approach even more closely to the irrationality of dumb animals they would not sin, according to the writers of theology. I wish you would think over for me, you wise fool, how by night and by day your soul is torn by so many carking cares; I wish you would gather into one heap all the discommodities of your life: then you will begin to understand from how many evils I have delivered my fools. Remember also that they are continually merry, they play, sing, and laugh; and what is more, they bring to others, wherever they may come, pleasure, jesting, sport, and laughter, as if they were created, by a merciful dispensation of the gods, for this one purpose—to drive away the sadness of human life.

Thus it comes about that, in a world where men are differently affected toward each other, all are at one in their attitude toward these innocents; all seek them out, give them food, keep them warm, embrace them, and give them aid, if occasion rises; and all grant them leave to say and to do what they wish, with impunity. So true it is that no one wishes to hurt them that even wild beasts, by a certain natural sense of their innocence, will refrain from doing them harm. They are indeed held sacred by the gods, especially by me; and not impiously do all men pay such honor to them. Thus kings find such consummate pleasure in my naturals that they cannot eat, or go on a progress, or even pass an hour, without them. The fact is that in some degree they prefer these simpletons to their crabbed wise men, whom yet they support for dignity's sake. That kings have this preference ought not, I suggest, seem remarkable or difficult of explanation: the wise men make a habit of bringing before them only serious matters, and, confident in their learning, will not fear at times "to grate their tender ears with rasping truths"; but fools furnish the one kind of thing that rulers are glad to get from any quarter and in any shape—jests, japes, laughter, pastime.

Notice also this estimable gift of fools, that they alone are frank and ingenuous. What is more praiseworthy than truth? Granted that the proverb of Alcibiades in Plato attributes truth to drunkards and children, yet all its merit is peculiarly mine, even as Euripides witnesses; his famous saying has come down to us: "A fool speaks foolish things." Whatever a fool has in his heart, that he sets also in his face and utters in his speech. But your wise man has two tongues, as this same Euripides mentions, one used for speaking truth, the other for speaking what he judges most opportune at the moment. Black is turned into white by these men of wisdom; they blow hot and cold with the same breath, and hidden in the breast they have something quite different from what they frame in speech. With all their felicity, indeed, the princes of earth seem to me most unfortunate in this respect, that they have no one to tell them the truth, but are compelled to have toadies instead of friends. But, some one will say, the ears of princes have an antipathy to truth, and for this reason the princes shun wise counsellors, fearing that possibly one more free than the others will stand forth and dare to speak things true rather than pleasant. Yes, by and large, veracity is disliked by kings. And yet a remarkable thing happens in the experience of my fools: from them not only true things, but even sharp reproaches, will be listened to; so that a statement which, if it came from a wise man's mouth, might be a capital offense, coming from a fool gives rise to incredible delight. Veracity, you know, has a certain authentic power of giving pleasure, if nothing offensive goes with it: but this the gods have granted only to fools. And for more or less the same reasons women are wont to take vast delight in men of this class, women being by nature more inclined to pleasure and toys. And however they may carry on with fools, even if it begins to wax a little too serious, they pass it off as a joke or a game—for the sex is ingenious, especially in veiling its own lapses.

Let me return to the topic of the happiness of fools. After a life lived out in much jollity, with no fear of death, or sense of it, they go straight to the Elysian Fields, there to entertain the pious and idle shades with their jests. Let us go about, then, and compare the lot of the wise man with that of the fool. Fancy some pattern of wisdom to put up against him, a man who wore out his whole boyhood and youth in pursuing the learned disciplines. He wasted the pleasantest time of life in unintermitted watchings, cares, and studies; and through the remaining part of it he never tasted so much as a tittle of pleasure; always frugal, impecunious, sad, austere; unfair and strict toward himself, morose and unamiable to others; afflicted by pallor, leanness, invalidism, sore eyes, premature age and white hair; dying before his appointed day. By the way, what difference does it make when a man of that sort dies? He has never lived. There you have a clear picture of the wise man.

[in margin, handwritten: a picture of the wise man (also a self portrait)]

[18] But here those Stoic frogs begin to croak at me again. Nothing, they say, is sadder than madness; flagrant folly is either very near madness, or, what is more likely, it is the same thing. For what is madness but a wandering of the wits? (But they themselves wander the whole way.) Come now, with the Muses prospering us, we shall also tear this syllogism wide open. Subtly argued, indeed; but just as, in Plato, Socrates teaches us to make two Venuses by splitting the usual one, and two Cupids by cutting Cupid apart, so in this case it would behoove our dialecticians to distinguish madness from madness—at least if they wish to be thought sane themselves. For certainly all madness is not calamitous. Otherwise Horace would not have said, "Does a dear madness play upon me?" Nor would Plato have placed that friendly fury of poets, prophets, and lovers among the chief blessings of life. Nor would the Sibyl have spoken of the "insane labor" of Aeneas. The fact is that "madness" is a genus comprising two species: one the revenging Furies send secretly from hell whenever, with their snaky locks unbound, they put into the hearts of mortal men lust for war, or insatiable thirst for wealth, shameful and illicit love, parricide, incest, sacrilege, or any other bane the of sort; or when they hound the guilty and stricken soul with fiends or with torch-bearing goblins. The other kind is far different from this. It comes, you see, from me; and of all things is most to be desired. It is present whenever an amiable dotage of the mind at once frees the spirit from carking

cares and anoints it with a complex delight. And such a dotage of the mind Cicero, writing to Atticus, wished for as a special bounty of the gods, for thereby he could lose his sense of the great evils of the time. Nor was that Greek in Horace far afield, whose madness took the form of sitting alone in the theater all day long, laughing, applauding, cheering, because he thought fine tragedies were being acted before him (though nothing at all was on the stage); yet he conducted himself acceptably in other relations of life—"pleasant with his friends, kind to his wife, and so indulgent to his servants that they might open a bottle of his wine without his going into a rage." When the care of his family and medical treatment had driven away these fits, and he was fully restored to himself, he protested to his friends. "By Pollux, you have killed me, not saved me," he said, "taking away my enjoyments this way and destroying by force the very pleasant illusion of my mind." And rightly; for they were themselves doting and had more need for hellebore, when they looked upon such a lucky and pleasant delusion as a disease to be driven out by potions.

[19] To be sure, I have not yet decided whether every deviation of the senses or the faculties ought to be called by the name of madness. To a man with weak eyes a mule may seem to be an ass; another man may admire some vulgar song as the finest poetry; neither will forthwith be considered mad. But a man who is deceived not only in his senses but also in the judgment of his mind, and this beyond what is ordinary, and upon all occasions, is bound to be considered as close to madness; if, for example, he thinks he is listening to a fine orchestra whenever he hears an ass braying; or if some beggar, born to low station, be-

lieves himself to be Croesus, King of the Lydians. And yet this kind of madness, assuming, as is usually the case, that it tends to give pleasure, can bring a delight above the common both to those who are seized by it and to those who look on but are not mad in the same way. This variety of madness is much more widespread than people generally realize. Thus one madman laughs at another, turn about, and they minister to each other's mutual pleasure. You will often see it happen that the madder man laughs more uproariously at the one who is not so mad.

The fact is that the more ways a man is deluded, the happier he is, if Folly is any judge. Only let him remain in that kind of madness which is peculiarly my own, and which is so widespread that I do not know whether out of the whole world of mortals it is possible to find one who is wise at all times of day, and who is not subject to some extravagance. It may be only that a man seeing a pumpkin believes it is a woman, and others give him the epithet of "mad," simply because so few people share his belief. But when another man swears roundly that his wife (whom he holds in common with many others) is a Penelope, only more virtuous, and thus flatters himself in the key of C-major, happily deluded; nobody calls him mad, because they see that this happens to other husbands here and there.

To this order belong the fellows who renounce everything else in favor of hunting wild game, and protest they feel an ineffable pleasure in their souls whenever they hear the raucous blast of the horns and the yelping of the hounds. Even the dung of the dogs, I am sure, smells like cinnamon to them. And what is so sweet as a beast being butchered? Cutting up bulls and oxen is properly given over to the humble plebeian, but it is a crime for game to be slaughtered except by a gentleman! There, with his head bared, on bended knees, with a knife designed just for this (for it is sacrilege to use any other), with certain ceremonial gestures he cuts just the proper members in the approved order. The company stands in silence, wondering as at some great novelty, although it has seen the same spectacle a thousand times. And if some bit of the animal is handed one of them to taste, he thinks he has gone up a step or so in the ranks of nobility. And thus with their butchering and eating of beasts they accomplish nothing at all unless it be to degenerate into beasts themselves, though they think, all the while, they are living the life of a king.

Very like to these is the class of men who suffer from an incurable itch to be abuilding. They transform round structures into square ones, and presently square ones into round ones. Nor is there any limit, any moderation, in this until by dint of having built themselves into utter poverty, they have nowhere to live and nothing to eat. What then? No matter, they have passed a number of years in complete happiness.

Next to these, it seems to me, come those who keep on trying, by new and secret skills, to transmute the forms of things, and who ransack earth and sea for a certain fifth essence. A honeyed hope cajoles them, so that they begrudge no pains or costs, but with marvellous ingenuity contrive that by which they may deceive themselves; and they go on in this pleasant imposture till, having gone through their possessions, there is not enough left to build a new furnace. Even then they do not leave off dreaming their pleasant dreams, but with all their strength they urge others to seek the same happiness. And when at last they are robbed of all hope, there remains this sentiment as a great solace, "In great things 'tis enough to have tried." Then they complain that life is too brief and does not suffice for the magnitude of their project.

As for gamblers, I have some doubt whether they should be admitted to our college. And yet it is a foolish and wholly ridiculous sight to see some of these addicts; as soon as they hear the rattle of the dice, their hearts leap and begin to beat faster. When, drawn further and further by hope of winning, they have made a wreck of all their resources, splitting the ship on Dice-Box Rock (which is even more deadly than the promontory Malea), and have just come through with their shirts, they choose to defraud anyone else but the winner, for fear they will get the reputation of not being men of their word. And what about those old gamesters, half-blind, who have to wear spectacles to play at all? At the last, when a justly earned gout has tied their joints in knots, they hire an assistant to put the dice into the box for them. A sweet business, indeed, were it not that the game usually passes over into an angry quarrel, so that it appertains to the Furies, not to me.

Here is a sort of men who beyond any doubt bear my trademark wholly—the ones who find joy in either hearing or telling monstrous lies and strange wonders. They never get enough of such stories, so long as prodigies are recounted, involving banshees, goblins, devils, or the like. The farther these are from the truth, the more they tickle the ears of our friends with pleasing sensations. These wonders serve very well to lighten tedious hours, but they also provide a way to make money, particularly for priests and pardoners.

[20] And next to these come the folk who have arrived at the foolish but gratifying belief that if they gaze on a picture of Polyphemus-Christopher they will not die that day, or that whoever salutes in certain prescribed words an image of Barbara will come through a battle unharmed, or that by making application to Erasmus on certain days, using a certain kind of candles and certain prayers, one will shortly become rich. Indeed, they have discovered another Hercules, and even another Hippolytus, in George; whose horse, piously decked out with trappings and bosses, they all but worship, often commending themselves to him by some little gift; while to swear by St. George's brass helmet is an oath for a king. Then what shall I say of the people who so happily fool themselves with forged pardons for sins, measuring out time to be spent in purgatory as if with an hour-glass, and figuring its centuries, years, months, days, and hours as if from a mathematical table, beyond possibility of error? Or I might speak of those who will promise themselves any and every thing, relying upon certain charms or prayers devised by some pious impostor either for his soul's sake or for money, to bring them wealth, reputation, pleasure, plenty, good health, long life, and a green old age, and at last a seat next to Christ's in heaven—but they do not wish to get it too soon. That is to say, when the pleasures of this life have finally failed them, willy-nilly, though they struggled tooth and nail to hold on to them, then it is time for the bliss of heaven to arrive.

I fancy that I see some merchant or soldier or judge laying down one small coin from his extensive booty and expecting that the whole cesspool of his life will be at once purified. He conceives that just so many perjuries, so many lustful acts, so many debauches, so many fights, murders, frauds, lies, and so many breaches of faith, are bought off as by contract; and so bought off that with a clean slate he may start from scratch upon a new round of sins. And who are more foolish, yet who more happy, than those who promise themselves something more than the highest felicity if they daily recite those seven verses of the *Psalms?* The seven, I mean, which some devil, a playful one, but blabbing rather than crafty, is believed to have pointed out to St. Bernard after he had been duped by the saint's trick. Things like that are so foolish, you know, that I am almost ashamed of them myself; yet they stand approved not only by the common people but even by teachers of religion. And is it not almost as bad when the several countries each lay claim to a particular saint of their own, and then assign particular powers respectively to the various saints and observe for each one his own peculiar rites of worship? One saint assists in time of toothache, another is propitious to women in travail, another recovers stolen goods, a fourth stands by with help in a shipwreck, and still another keeps the sheep in good repair; and so of the rest, though it would take too long to specify all of them. Some of them are good for a number of purposes, particularly the Virgin Mother, to whom the common people tend to attribute more than to the Son.

Yet what do men ask of these saints except things that pertain to folly? Think a bit: among all those consecrated gifts which you see covering the walls of some churches, and even hung on the ceiling, do you ever find one given in gratitude for an escape from folly, or because the giver has been made any whit wiser? One person has come safe to land. A second survived being run through in a duel. One no less fortunately than bravely got away from a battlefield, leaving the rest to fight. Another was brought near to the gallows, but by favor of some saint who is friendly to thieves he has decided that he should go on relieving those who are burdened with too much wealth. Another escaped in a jail-break. Another came through a fever, in spite of his doctor. The poisoned drink of another, by loosening his bowels, served to cure him instead of kill him, not at all to the joy of his wife, who lost both her labor and her expenses. Another's cart was turned over, but he drove both horses home safely. Another was dug out of the debris of a fallen house. Another, caught in the act by a husband, made good his escape. No one gives thanks for a recovery from being a fool. So sweet it is not to be wise that mortal men will pray to be delivered from anything sooner than from Folly.

But why should I launch out upon this ocean of superstition? "For if I had a hundred tongues, a hundred mouths, a voice of brass, I could not set forth all the shapes of fools or run over all the names of folly." Yet the whole life of Christian folk everywhere is full of fanaticisms of this kind. Our priests allow them, without regret, and even foster them, being aware of how much money is wont to accrue from this source. In this posture of affairs, suppose that some odious wise man were to step up and sing out this, which is true: "You will not die badly if you live well. You get quit of your sins if you add to the money payment a hatred of evil-doing, add tears, watchings, prayers, fastings; and if you alter the whole basis of your life. This or that saint will be gracious to you if you emulate his goodness." If the wise man, I say, were to start howling out things like that, just see from what contentment, and into what a turmoil, he would all of a sudden drive the souls of men!

To this college of ours belong those who, while they are living, scrupulously arrange the funeral ceremonies with which they desire to be laid away, prescribing exactly how many candles, how many mourners, how many singers, and how many hired pallbearers they wish to have there. It is precisely as if they expected that some capacity for appreciating the spectacle would come back to them, or that, lying dead, they would feel ashamed if the body was not laid away in grand style. They are as zealous about the matter as if they had been made aediles, charged with providing shows and feasts.

Although I must hasten on, I cannot pass over in silence those who, while differing in no respect from the meanest tinker, flatter themselves beyond measure with the empty title of nobility. One will trace his family back to Aeneas, one to Brutus, and a third to King Arthur. In every room they display pictures and busts of their ancestors. They specify their grandfathers and great-grandfathers, and have by heart the ancient names, while all the time they are not so different from senseless statues themselves and are worth, it may be, less than the ones they show off. Yet by virtue of my lovely companion Philautia, they lead a pleasant life. There will always be other fools, too, to admire specimens of this breed as if they were gods.

[21] Why speak of this or that contingent, however, as if Lady Philautia did not everywhere and among all ranks

use her wonderful skills to make men happy as happy can
be? Though this man is uglier than an ape, obviously he
seems a Nireus to himself. This one, drawing three lines
with a compass, thinks himself a Euclid; this other, as
musical as "an ass with a lyre," though "he sounds worse
than a cock treading a hen," believes that he sings like
another Hermogenes. But of all madness, that is sweetest
whereby a person glories in some useful gift possessed by
members of his household as if it were his own. Such was
that doubly blessed rich man in Seneca: whenever he
told a story, he had a brace of servants at hand to prompt
him on the names. Though a man otherwise so weak that
he could scarcely keep alive, he would not hesitate to get
into a fist-fight, relying on the circumstance that he had a
lot of stout fellows in his entourage.

What need we say about practitioners in the arts? Self-
love is the hallmark of them all. You will find that they
would sooner give up their paternal acres than any piece
of their poor talents. Take particularly actors, singers,
orators, and poets; the more unskilled one of them is, the
more insolent he will be in his self-satisfaction, the more
he will blow himself up, and spread himself. And "like
lips find like lettuce"; indeed, the more absurd a thing is,
the more admirers it collects. Thus the worst art pleases
the most people, for the simple reason that the larger part
of mankind, as I said before, is subject to folly. If, therefore, the less skilled man is more pleasing both in his own
eyes and in the wondering gaze of the many, what reason
is there that he should prefer sound discipline and true
skill? In the first place, these will cost him a great outlay;
in the second place, they will make him more affected

and meticulous; and finally, they will please far fewer of his audience.

And now I see that it is not only in individual men that nature has implanted self-love. She implants a kind of it as a common possession in the various races, and even cities. By this token the English claim, besides a few other things, good looks, music, and the best eating as their special properties. The Scots flatter themselves on the score of high birth and royal blood, not to mention their dialectical skill. Frenchmen have taken all politeness for their province; though the Parisians, brushing all others aside, also award themselves the prize for knowledge of theology. The Italians usurp *belles lettres* and eloquence; and they all flatter themselves upon the fact that they alone, of all mortal men, are not barbarians. In this particular point of happiness the Romans stand highest, still dreaming pleasantly of ancient Rome. The Venetians are blessed with a belief in their own nobility. The Greeks, as well as being the founders of the learned disciplines, vaunt themselves upon their titles to the famous heroes of old. The Turks, and that whole rabble of the truly barbarous, claim praise for their religion, laughing at Christians as superstitious. And what is much more pleasant, the Jews still are awaiting their own Messiah, and even today hold on to their Moses with might and main. Spaniards yield to no one in martial reputation. Germans take pride in their great stature and their knowledge of magic.

But not to pursue details, I am sure you observe how Philautia is the parent of delight for men, in particular and in general; and her sister Flattery is almost as fruitful. Indeed, Philautia is nothing but a cajoling of one's own self; do the same thing to someone else, and it becomes Kolakia. Nowadays this adulation is in bad odor, but only among those who are more concerned about names of things than things themselves. They have the notion that bad faith is inseparable from adulation; but the examples of dumb animals, even, could show them how far they are wrong. What is more fawning than a dog? And yet what is more faithful? What is more fond and caressing than a squirrel? But where will you find a better friend to man? Unless, perhaps, it seems to you that fierce lions, pitiless tigers, or fiery leopards stand humanity in better stead. To be sure, there is a baneful kind of flattery by which certain traitors and mockers drive their wretched victims to destruction. But this of mine proceeds from a certain kindness and candor of mind, and is much nearer to virtue than is what stands opposite to it—asperity, or what Horace calls "uncomely and heavy moroseness." My flattery raises the dejected spirit, it soothes those who are grieving, freshens the faint, quickens the dull, eases the suffering, mollifies the fierce, joins loves together and keeps them so joined. It allures childhood to pursue the study of literature, it cheers the old, and, under the color of praise, it warns and instructs princes without offense. In brief, it acts to make every man more pleasing and more dear to himself; this is indeed the main point of happiness. What is more gracious than the way two mules scratch each other? Meanwhile, I shall not go on to tell how this flattery bears a great part in your famous eloquence, a greater part in medicine, and the greatest part of all in poetry. To conclude, it is honey and spice of all human intercourse.

MAN HUGS DELUSION

[22] But it is a sad thing, they say, to be deceived. No; the saddest thing is not to be deceived. For they are quite beside the mark who think that the happiness of a man is to be found in things, as such; it resides in opinion. For such is the obscurity and variety of human affairs that nothing can be clearly known, as has been correctly said by my Academics, the least impudent of the philosophers. Or if something can be known, usually it is something that makes against the enjoyment of life. Finally, the mind of man is so constructed that it is taken far more with disguises than with realities. If anyone wants to make a convincing and easy test of this, let him go to church and listen to sermons. If something solid is being said, everybody sleeps, or yawns, or is ill at ease. But if the bawler—I made a slip, I meant to say prater—as they so often do, begins some old wives' tale, everybody awakens, straightens up, and gapes for it. Also if there is a somewhat fabulous or poetical saint (and if you want an example, imagine George or Christopher or Barbara to belong to this class), you will see him honored much more religiously than Peter or Paul or even Christ himself. But these things do not belong here.

Yet how little this addition to happiness costs! whereas it is necessary to lay out a much greater price for almost any of the solid things, even for the poorest of them— grammar, for instance. But opinion is picked up very easily, and yet for all that, it conduces far more to happiness. Suppose a man is eating some rotten kippers, and the man beside him cannot abide the smell of them; but to the eater they taste and smell like ambrosia. I ask you, what is the consequence, as regards happiness? On the other hand, if the best sturgeon turns your stomach, what can it contribute to the blessedness of existence? If a man has a wife who is notoriously ugly, yet who seems to her husband fit to enter a competition with Venus herself, is it not the same as if she were truly beautiful? If one was to behold a canvas daubed with red lead and mud, and to admire it under the persuasion that it was a picture by Apelles or Zeuxis, would he not be happier than another who buys the work of such masters at a high price, but feels less of pleasure, perhaps, in viewing it? I know a man of my name who gave his young wife some imitation jewels as a present, persuading her—for he is a plausible joker—that they were not only genuine and natural but also of unique and inestimable value. Pray tell me, what difference did it make to the girl, so long as she joyously delighted her eyes and heart with glass, and carefully kept these trinkets in a safe place never far from her person? In the meantime, her husband had avoided expense, he had enjoyed his wife's delusion, and he had bound her to himself no less than as if he had given greater purchases. In your judgment, what difference is there between those who in Plato's cave look admiringly at the shadows and simulacra of various things, desiring nothing, quite well satisfied with themselves, as against the wise man who emerges from the cave and sees realities? If Micyllus, in Lucian, had been allowed always to go on dreaming that rich and golden dream, there would have been no reason for him to choose any other happiness.

Hence there either is no difference or, if there is difference, the state of fools is to be preferred. First, their happiness costs least. It costs only a bit of illusion. And second, they enjoy it in the company of so many others. The possession of no good thing is welcome without a companion. And who has not heard of the paucity of wise men—if indeed any is to be found. Out of several centuries the Greeks counted seven altogether; yet, so help me, if one were to canvass them with care and accuracy, may I be shot if he would find so much as one half-wise man—nay, so much as one-third of one wise man!

[23] You recall that among the many glories of Bacchus this is held to be chief, that he washes away the cares of the soul. Yet it is for a short time only, for as soon as you sleep off his fumes, the cares of the soul come galloping back, riding four white horses, as the saying is. How much more bounteous and more prompt is my boon! For I fill the mind with a sort of perpetual drunkenness; I glut it with joys, dear delights, and gay fancies; and this without any formalities or difficulties. I have seen to it that no man alive should be without my blessing; but the gifts of the other deities come with partiality, certain ones to certain people. Not everywhere, for instance, is produced the rich and mild wine "which drives away cares, and attends upon opulent hope." Beauty of face, the gift of Venus, is granted to few; eloquence, the gift of Mercury, to still fewer. Not many, by having the favor of Hercules, get riches. Homer's Jupiter does not bestow upon just anyone the rule of kingdoms. Often Mars favors neither army. Many depart sad from Apollo's tripod. Jove often thunders. Apollo sometimes sends pestilence on his arrows. Neptune drowns more than he saves. And of course I might make mention of the anti-Joves, of Pluto, Ate, Poena, Febris, and their kind—no gods at all but hangmen. It is only I, Folly, who embrace all men without distinction in my provident goodness. Nor do I wait for

prayers. I am not pettish, demanding expiations if some ceremony has been overlooked. Nor do I throw heaven and earth into an uproar if someone has issued an invitation to the other gods, but has left me at home, not allowing me to partake of the smoke of their sacrifices. The fact is that the captiousness of the other gods is such that one is likely to get along better, and is even safer, if he neglects them entirely, than if he undertakes to worship them properly. There are men like that, so hard to please and so sensitive to injury that it pays better to hold them as utter strangers than to have any familiarity with them.

But they tell us that nobody sacrifices, or builds a temple, to Folly. Yes, and I am amazed, as I said before, at such ingratitude. Yet in my easy-going way I take this in good part, though I could scarcely complain, with any grace, about the lack of such attentions; for why should I demand incense or meal or a he-goat or a she-hog, when men in all parts of the world unanimously accord me that kind of worship which is specially approved by our divines? Maybe I ought to envy Diana, because she is appeased by human blood! No, I consider that I am most piously worshipped when men—and they all do it—take me to their souls, manifest me in their actions, and represent me in their lives. This kind of worship of the saints is extremely rare among Christians. Plenty of them will burn a little candle to the Virgin Mother, and this at noon when it is unnecessary; but how few burn with zeal to imitate her in chastity of life, temperance, love of heavenly things! For this, at the last, is true worship, by far most pleasing to those above. Besides, what should I want of a temple, when the universal world is my temple, and, if I mistake not, a goodly one? Nor are communicants lacking—except where men are lacking. I am not so foolish as to ask stone images, painted up in colors; they would but hinder the worship of me, since by the stupid and dull those figures are worshipped instead of the saints themselves. And it would come about with me exactly as it usually does with the saints—they are thrown out of doors by their substitutes. I consider that I have many statues erected to me, as many as there are mortals who bear my living presentment in their faces, even if it is against their will. Hence I have no reason to envy the other gods if one or the other is worshipped in some particular corner of the earth, and that on stated days only—as, for instance, Phoebus is worshipped in Rhodes, Venus in Cyprus, Juno at Argos, Minerva at Athens, Jupiter on Olympus, Neptune at Tarentum, Priapus at Lampsacus—so long as I have the entire world zealously offering far greater sacrifices to me.

[24] And if I should seem at this point to be speaking more rashly than truly, I suggest that for a time we shall look into the lives of men, and it will be apparent how much they owe to me and how many, the greatest along with the humble, follow me. We shall not run over the lives of everybody, for that would take too long, but only the most notable; from which it will be easy to form an opinion about the others. For why should I spend time on the common and baser sort, who are wholly mine beyond controversy? They everywhere teem with so many forms of folly and daily devise so many new ones that a thousand Democrituses would not suffice for laughing at them—and there would be work, then, for one more Democritus to laugh at the laughers.

You would never believe what sport and entertainment your mortal manikins provide daily for the gods. These gods, you know, set aside their sober forenoon hours for composing quarrels and giving ear to prayers. But after that, when they are well moistened with nectar and have no desire for the transaction of business, they seek out some promontory of heaven and, sitting there with faces bent downward, they watch what mortal men are adoing. There is no show like it. Good God, what a theater! How various the action of fools! (I may say that now and then I take a seat alongside the gods of the poets.) Here is a fellow dying for love of a sweet young thing, and the less he is loved in return, the more helplessly he is in love. This one marries a dowry, not a wife. This one prostitutes his own wife. The jealousy of another keeps watch like Argus. Here is a man in mourning, but mercy me, what fool things he says and does! Hiring mourners as if they were actors, to play a comedy of grief! Another man squeezes out a tear at the tomb of his mother-in-law. This one spends on his belly whatever he can scrape together by hook or crook, but presently he will be just as hungry again. Another finds nothing better than sleep and idleness. There are those who get themselves into a stew working at what is other people's business, while they neglect their own. There is also the broker, who accounts himself rich on other people's money, but is on the way to bankruptcy. Another thinks that the happy life consists in living like a pauper in order that his heir may be wealthy. Another, for the sake of a small and uncertain profit, sails the seven seas, exposing his life, which no money could pay for, to the hazard of waves and winds. This one prefers seeking riches in war to passing a safe and quiet life at home. Some decide that they can most conveniently attain to wealth by courting and fawning upon childless old men. There are even those who prefer to do the same to rich old women. Both kinds furnish rare sport to the gods who are spectators, because they are usually cheated by the parties they set out to catch.

But the most foolish and sordid of all are your merchants, in that they carry on the most sordid business of all and this by the most sordid methods; for on occasion they lie, they perjure themselves, they steal, they cheat, they impose on the public. Yet they make themselves men of importance—because they have gold rings on their fingers. Nor do they lack for flattering friars who admire them and call them Right Honorable in public, with the purpose, surely, that some little driblet from the ill-gotten gains may flow to themselves. Elsewhere you will see certain Pythagoreans, in whose eyes all things are common—to such a degree, in fact, that whatever they light upon that is lying around loose they carry off with a tranquil spirit, as if it passed to them by inheritance. There are others who are rich only in wishes; they build beautiful air-castles and conceive that doing so is enough for happiness. Some delight in passing for wealthy men away from home, though they starve meanly enough in their own houses. One man hastens to put into circulation what money he has; his neighbor hoards his up through thick and thin. This one pushes forward as a candidate for public honors; that one finds his pleasure by his fireside. A good many people bring suits which are destined never to end; once and again they eagerly strive to outdo each other—in enriching the judge who sets the postponements and the advocate who colludes with him.

One burns with zeal for revolutions; another is toiling upon his Grand Scheme. This man leaves wife and children at home and sets out on a pilgrimage to Jerusalem, Rome, or the shrine of St. James, where he has no particular business. In sum, if you might look down from the moon, as Menippus did of old, upon the numberless agitations among mortal men, you would think you were seeing a swarm of flies or gnats, quarreling among themselves, waging wars, setting snares for each other, robbing, sporting, wantoning, being born, growing old, and dying. And one can scarce believe what commotions and what tragedies this animalcule, little as he is and so soon to perish, sets agoing. For sometimes a trivial war or a spell of the plague will sweep off and utterly wipe out thousands of them at once.

[25] But I should be most foolish myself and worthy of the manifold laughter of Democritus, if I should go on counting forms of folly and madness among the folk. Let me turn to those who maintain among mortals an appearance of wisdom and, as the saying is, seek for the golden bough. Among these the grammarians hold first place. Nothing could be more calamity-stricken, nothing more afflicted, than this generation of men, nothing so hated of God, if I were not at hand to mitigate the pains of their wretched profession by a certain sweet infusion of madness. For they are not only liable to the five curses which the Greek epigram calls attention to in Homer, but indeed to six hundred curses; as being hunger-starved and dirty in their schools—I said "their schools," but it were better said "their knowledge-factories" or "their mills" or even "their shambles"—among herds of boys. There they grow old with their labors, they are deafened by the

noise, they sicken by reason of the stench and nastiness. Yet thanks to me, they see themselves as first among men; so greatly do they please themselves when they terrify the timorous band by a menacing look and tone; when they beat the little wretches with ferules, rods, or straps; and when, imitating the ass in Aesop, they storm fiercely in all directions, as whim may dictate. And do you know, all the dirtiness seems sheer elegance, the stench is perfume of sweet marjoram, and the miserable servitude considered to be a kingdom, such a one that they would not trade their tyranny for the empire of Phalaris or Dionysius.

But nowadays they are especially happy in their new illusion of being learned. Of course they cram their pupils with utter nonsense, but, good Lord, what Palemon, what Donatus, do they not scorn in comparison with themselves! I do not know by what sleight of hand they work it so well, but to the foolish mothers and addlepated fathers of their pupils they seem to be just what they make themselves out to be. On top of this they have another pleasure. When one of them can drag out of some worm-eaten manuscript such a fact as the name of Anchises' mother or some word not generally known, such as *bubsequa*, *bovinator*, or *manticulator;* or if one can dig up somewhere a fragment of an ancient tombstone with an inscription badly worn away—O Jupiter! what exulting then, what triumphs, what panegyrics, as if they had conquered Africa or captured Babylon.

As for those stilted, insipid verses they display on all occasions (and there are those to admire them), obviously the writer believes that the soul of Virgil has transmigrated into his own breast. But the funniest sight of all is to see them admiring and praising each other, trading compliment for compliment, thus mutually scratching each other's itch. Yet if one commits a lapse in a single word, and another more quick-sighted by happy chance lights on it, O Hercules, what a stir presently, what scufflings, what insults, what invectives! May I have the ill-will of the whole grammatical world, if I lie. I used to know a certain polymath versed in Greek, Latin, mathematics, philosophy, and medicine, and a master of them all, then some sixty years old; laying aside all the others, he vexed and tortured himself with grammar for more than twenty years, deeming that he would be happy if he were allowed to live until he had settled with certainty how the eight parts of speech are to be distinguished, a thing which none of the Greeks or Latins succeeded in doing definitively. It becomes a matter to be put to the test of battle, when someone makes a conjunction of a word which belongs in the bailiwick of the adverbs. Thanks to this, there are as many grammars as there are grammarians—nay, more; for my friend Aldus single-handed produced grammars on more than five occasions. He has overlooked no work of the kind, however barbarously and tediously written; he has expounded each, and criticized each; jealous of everybody who may be toiling, however ineptly, in the same field, and pitiably in fear that, with some one else snatching the glory, his labor of many years will be lost. Do you prefer to call this madness or folly? It is no great matter to me; only confess that it is done with my assistance; so that a creature otherwise by far the most wretched of all is raised to such happiness that he would not wish to exchange his lot for that of the kings of Persia.

POETS AND RHETORICIANS

The poets owe less to me, though by their own avowal they are of my faction, being a race of free souls (as the proverb has it), all of whose efforts tend to no other end than soothing the ears of fools with vapid trifles and silly stories. And yet they so rely on these things, strange to say, that they not only promise themselves immortality, and a life equal to that of the gods, but they also assure as much to others. Philautia and Kolakia are more intimate with this fraternity than with others, nor am I worshipped by any tribe of men more sincerely or with greater constancy. As for the rhetoricians, though they sometimes play both sides against the middle, and collude with the philosophers, they are also of my party, on many counts, although this chiefly proves it: besides much other nonsense, they have written so critically and so much on the method of joking. Whoever he was who wrote the art of rhetoric *Ad Herennium* includes folly itself as one species of humor; and in the work of Quintilian, easily the prince of this realm, there is a chapter longer than the *Iliad* on the subject of raising laughter. In general they allow this much to folly, that many times what cannot be refuted by arguments can be parried by laughter. But you may think that exciting laughter by witty remarks, and this by a set method, does not belong to Folly.

[26] Of the same brand also are those who pursue fame by turning out books. All of them are highly indebted to me, but especially those who blacken paper with sheer triviality. For the ones who write learnedly for the verdict of a few scholars, not ruling out even a Persius or a Laelius as judge, seem to me more pitiable than happy, since they continuously torture themselves:

they add, they alter, they blot something out, they put it back in, they do their work over, they recast it, they show it to friends, they keep it for nine years; yet they never satisfy themselves. At such a price they buy an empty reward, namely, praise—and that the praise of a handful. They buy it with such an expense of long hours, so much loss of that sweetest of all things, sleep, so much sweat, so many vexations. Add also the loss of health, the wreck of their good looks, weakness of eyes or even blindness, poverty, malice, denial of pleasures, premature old age, and early death—and if there are other things like these, add them. The scholar considers himself compensated for such ills when he wins the approbation of one or two other weak-eyed scholars. But my author is crazy in a far happier way, since without any prolonged thought he quickly puts in writing whatever has come into his head or chanced to his pen, even his dreams; and all this with little waste of paper, knowing that if the trifles he has written are trivial enough the greater number of readers—that is, the fools and ignoramuses—will approve. Of what consequence is it to ignore the two or three scholars, even if they chance to read the work? Or what weight will the censure of a few learned men have, as against the great multitude of those who will shout acclaim?

But the wiser writers are those who put out the work of others as their own. By a few strokes of the pen they transfer to their own account the glory which was the fruit of much toil on another's part, drawing comfort from the thought that even if it should happen that they are publicly convicted of plagiarism, meanwhile they shall have enjoyed for a period the emoluments of authorship. It is worth one's while to see how pleased authors are with themselves when they are popular, and pointed out in a crowd—"There is a celebrity!" Their work is on display in booksellers' shops, with three cryptic words in large type on the title-page, preferably foreign words, something like a magician's spell. Ye gods! What are all these things but words, after all? Few people will ever hear of them, in comparison with the total population of the world, and far fewer will admire them, since there is such divergence of tastes, even among the vulgar. And why is it that the very names of the authors are often invented, or taken from the books of the ancients? One of them likes to sign himself Telemachus, another Stelenus or Laertes, this one Polycrates, that one Thrasymachus; so that nowadays it matters not if you ascribe your book to a chameleon or a gourd, or simply to *alpha* or *beta*, as the philosophers have a way of doing.

The daintiest thing is when they compliment each other, turn about, in an exchange of letters, verses, and puffs; fools praising fools and dunces praising dunces. The first, in the opinion of the second, is an Alcaeus; the second, in the opinion of the first, is a Callimachus. One puts another far above Cicero; the other then finds the one more learned than Plato. Or sometimes they will pick out a competitor and increase their reputation through rivalry with him. As a result, the doubtful public is split into opposing camps, until, when the battle is well over, each leaves the field as victor and each has a triumphal parade. Wise men deride all this as most foolish, as indeed it is. Who denies it? But meanwhile, by my boon our authors lead a sweet life, nor would they exchange their triumphs for those of the Scipios. And while the scholars indeed have a great deal of fun laughing at them, and savor to the full the madnesses of others, they themselves owe a good deal to me, which they cannot disavow without being the most ungrateful of men.

[27] Among men of learned professions, the lawyers may claim first place for themselves, nor is there any other class quite so self-satisfied; for while they industriously roll up the stone of Sisyphus by dint of weaving together six hundred laws in the same breath, no matter how little to the purpose, and by dint of piling glosses upon glosses and opinions upon opinions, they contrive to make their profession seem the most difficult of all. What is really tedious commends itself to them as brilliant. Let us put in with them the logicians and sophists, a breed of men more loquacious than the famed brass kettles at Dodona; any one of them can out-chat twenty picked women. They would be happier, however, if they were merely talkative, and not quarrelsome as well, to such a degree that they will stubbornly cut and thrust over a lock of goat's wool, quite losing track of the truth in question while they go on disputing. Their self-love makes them happy, and equipped with three syllogisms they will unhesitatingly dare to join battle upon any subject with any man. Mere frowardness brings them back unbeaten, though you match Stentor against them.

Near these march the scientists, reverenced for their beards and the fur on their gowns, who teach that they alone are wise while the rest of mortal men flit about as shadows. How pleasantly they dote, indeed, while they construct their numberless worlds, and measure the sun, moon, stars, and spheres as with thumb and line. They assign causes for lightning, winds, eclipses, and other inexplicable things, never hesitating a whit, as if they were privy to the secrets of nature, artificer of things, or as if they visited us fresh from the council of the gods. Yet all the while nature is laughing grandly at them and their conjectures. For to prove that they have good intelligence of nothing, this is a sufficient argument: they can never explain why they disagree with each other on every subject. Thus knowing nothing in general, they profess to know all things in particular; though they are ignorant even of themselves, and on occasion do not see the ditch or the stone lying across their path, because many of them are blear-eyed or absent-minded; yet they proclaim that they perceive ideas, universals, forms without matter, primary substances, quiddities, and ecceities—things so tenuous, I fear, that Lynceus himself could not see them. When they especially disdain the vulgar crowd is when they bring out their triangles, quadrangles, circles, and mathematical pictures of the sort, lay one upon the other, intertwine them into a maze, then deploy some letters as if in line of battle, and presently do it over in reverse order—and all to involve the uninitiated in darkness. Their fraternity does not lack those who predict future events by consulting the stars, and promise wonders even more magical; and these lucky scientists find people to believe them.

[28] Perhaps it were better to pass over the theologians in silence, and not to move such a Lake Camarina, or to handle such an herb *Anagyris foetida*, as that marvellously supercilious and irascible race. For they may attack me with six hundred arguments, in squadrons, and drive me to make a recantation; which if I refuse, they will straightway proclaim me an heretic. By this thunderbolt they are

wont to terrify any toward whom they are ill-disposed. No other people are so loth to acknowledge my favors to them; yet the divines are bound to me by no ordinary obligations. They are happy in their self-love, and as if they already inhabited the third heaven they look down from a height on all other mortal men as on creatures that crawl on the ground, and they come near to pitying them. They are protected by a wall of scholastic definitions, arguments, corollaries, implicit and explicit propositions; they have so many hideaways that they could not be caught even by the net of Vulcan; for they slip out on their distinctions, by which also they cut through all knots as easily as with a double-bitted axe from Tenedos; and they abound with newly-invented terms and prodigious vocables. Furthermore, they explain as pleases them the most arcane matters, such as by what method the world was founded and set in order, through what conduits original sin has been passed down along the generations, by what means, in what measure, and how long the perfect Christ was in the Virgin's womb, and how accidents subsist in the Eucharist without their subject.

But those are hackneyed. Here are questions worthy of the great and (as some call them) illuminated theologians, questions to make them prick up their ears—if ever they chance upon them. Whether divine generation took place at a particular time? Whether there are several sonships in Christ? Whether this is a possible proposition: God the Father hates the Son? Whether God could have taken upon Himself the likeness of a woman? Or of a devil? Of an ass? Of a gourd? Of a piece of flint? Then how would that gourd have preached, performed miracles, or been crucified? Also, what would Peter have consecrated if he had administered the sacrament while Christ's body hung upon the Cross? Also whether at that moment Christ could be said to be a man? And whether after the resurrection it will be forbidden to eat and drink? (Now, while there is time, they are providing against hunger and thirst!) These finespun trifles are numberless, with others even more subtle, having to do with instants of time, notions, relations, accidents, quiddities, entities, which no one can perceive with his eyes unless, like Lynceus, he can see in blackest darkness things that are not there.

We must put in also those hard sayings, contradictions indeed, compared to which the Stoic maxims which were called paradoxes seem the merest simplicity. For instance: it is less of a crime to cut the throats of a thousand men than to set a stitch on a poor man's shoe on the Lord's day; it is better to choose that the universe should perish, body, boots, and breeches (as the saying is), than that one should tell a single lie, however inconsequential. The methods our scholastics pursue only render more subtle these subtlest of subtleties; for you will escape from a labyrinth more quickly than from the tangles of Realists, Nominalists, Thomists, Albertists, Occamists, Scotists—I have not named all, but the chief ones only. But in all these sects there is so much learning and so much difficulty that I should think the apostles themselves must needs have the help of some other spirit if they were to try disputing on these topics with our new generation of theologues.

Paul could exhibit faith; but when he said, "Faith is the substance of things hoped for, the evidence of things not seen," he did not define it doctorally. The same apostle, though he exemplified charity supremely well, divided and defined it with very little logical skill in his first epistle to the Corinthians, Chapter 13. And no doubt the apostles consecrated the Eucharist devoutly enough; but suppose you had questioned them about the *terminus a quo* and the *terminus ad quem*, or about transubstantiation—how the body is in many places at once, the difference between the body of Christ when in heaven, when on the Cross, when in the sacrament of the Eucharist, about the point when transubstantiation occurs (seeing that the prayer effecting it is a discrete quantity having extension in time)—they would not have answered with the same acuteness, I suggest, with which the sons of Scotus distinguish and define these matters. The apostles knew the mother of Jesus, but who among them has demonstrated philosophically just how she was kept clear from the sin of Adam, as our theologians have done? Peter received the keys, received them from One who did not commit them to an unworthy person, and yet I doubt that he ever understood—for Peter never did attain to subtlety—that a person who did not have knowledge could have the key to knowledge. They went about baptizing everywhere, and yet they never taught what is the formal, the material, the efficient, and the final cause of baptism, nor is mention made by them that it has both a delible character and an indelible one. They worshipped, to be sure, but in spirit, following no other teaching than that of the Gospel, "God is a spirit, and they that worship Him must worship Him in spirit and in truth." It seems never to have been revealed to them that a picture drawn with charcoal on a wall ought to be worshipped

with the same worship as Christ himself—at least if it is
drawn with two fingers outstretched and the hair un-
shorn, and has three sets of rays in the nimbus fastened to
the back of the head. For who would comprehend these
things if he had not consumed all of thirty-six years upon
the physics and metaphysics of Aristotle and the Scotists?

In similar wise, the apostles preach grace, and yet they
never determined what the difference is between grace
freely given and grace that makes one deserving. They
urge us to good works, but do not separate work, work
working, and work that has been worked. At all times
they inculcate charity, but do not distinguish charity
which is infused from that which is acquired, or explain
whether charity is an accident or a substance, created or
uncreated. They abhor sin, but may I be shot if they
could define scientifically what it is we call sin, unless
they had the luck to be instructed by the spirit of the
Scotists.

You can never make me believe that Paul, by whose
learning you can judge that of the others, would so often
have condemned questions, disputes, genealogies, and
what he called "strifes of words," if he had really been a
master of those subtleties, especially in view of the fact
that all the controversies of that time were mere little
backwoods debates, quite without art, when put into
comparison with the more than Chrysippean subtleties
of Our Masters. And yet these masters are as modest as
can be; for if by chance something was written by the
apostles carelessly or not quite doctorally, they do not
damn it out of hand, but give it a proper interpretation.
Thus much honor they pay, partly to the antiquity of the
passage and partly to the apostolic authority. And dear

me, it would be almost unjust to look for very scholarly things from the apostles, for they heard no word about them from their Master. But if a lapse of the same kind turns up in Chrysostom, Basil, or Jerome, it is enough for our scholars to jot down, "It is not accepted."

The apostles also confuted the heathen philosophers and the Jews, who are by nature the stubbornest of all, but they did so rather by their lives and miracles than by syllogisms; and of course they dealt with people not one of whom had wit enough to get through a single *quodlibet* of Scotus. Nowadays, what heathen or heretic does not yield at once in the face of these finespun subtleties? Unless, indeed, he is so dull that he cannot follow them or so impudent that he hisses them down, or possibly so well instructed in the same equivocations that the contest is an equal one. Then it is as if you were to match one magician against another, or as if someone with a charmed sword should fight with a man whose sword also happened to be charmed. It would be nothing but reweaving the web of Penelope. In my poor judgment Christians would be wiser if instead of their gross unwieldy battalions of soldiers, with which for some time now they have been warring without any particular favor from Mars, they would send against the Turks and Saracens these brawling Scotists and stubborn Occamists and invincible Albertists, along with the whole band of Sophists. Then, I am bold to think, they would witness a battle which would be the merriest ever fought, and a victory such as was never seen before. Who is so phlegmatic that the shrewdness of these fighters would not excite him? Who so stupid that such sophistries would not quicken him? Who so quick-sighted that they would not throw a mist before his eyes?

[29] But it seems to you I say all these things almost as a joke. No wonder, indeed, since among the divines themselves are some, instructed in sound learning, who are nauseated by what they deem the frivolous subtleties of theologues. There are those who abhor as a kind of sacrilege, and class as the greatest impiety, this speaking with unclean lips about holy things, which are rather to be worshipped than expounded; this disputing by the profane methods of the heathen; this arrogant way of defining; this defilement of the majesty of sacred theology by silly, sordid terms and sentiments. Yet for all that, the others please and even applaud themselves in their happiness, so busied night and day about their precious bagatelles that not enough time is left to allow them to open a gospel or the epistles of Paul. And while they fribble thus in the schools, they deem that they are holding up the universal church, otherwise about to fall in ruins, by the props of their syllogisms, exactly as Atlas, according to the poets, holds up the heavens on his shoulders. You can imagine how much pleasure it gives them to shape and reshape the Holy Scriptures as if they were made of wax; to demand that their own conclusions, subscribed to by a few schoolmen, shall be accounted greater than Solon's laws and preferred before a pope's decrees; and as censors of the world to force a retraction of anything that does not square, to a line, with their implicit as well as explicit conclusions. And these they announce like oracles. "This proposition is scandalous." "This one is lacking in reverence." "This savors of heresy." "This does not have the right ring." The inference is that

neither baptism nor the gospel nor Paul and Peter, nor Saints Jerome and Augustine, nay, not even the great Aristotelitotical Thomas himself, can make a Christian unless the vote of these baccalaureate sirs has been added as well. And what nicety in passing judgment! Who would ever have thought, if these wise men had not instructed us, that a man who approves as good Latin both *matula putes* and *matula putet*, or both *ollae fervere* and *ollam fervere*, is not a Christian? Who else would have purged the church from black errors of this sort—which no one would ever have had occasion to read about if these wise men had not published them under the great seals of their universities? Forsooth, are they not happy while they do these things?

Furthermore, they draw exact pictures of every part of hell as if they had spent many years in that commonwealth. They also fabricate new heavenly spheres as fancy dictates, adding the biggest of all and the finest—for there must be a suitable place for the souls of the blessed to take their walks in, to entertain at dinner, or even to play a game of ball. Their heads are so stuffed and stretched with these and two thousand other whim-whams of the same sort that I am sure Jupiter's cerebrum was not any more gravid when he yelled for Vulcan's help to bring forth Pallas. Wherefore do not be astonished when you see at a public disputation the head of one of them all bound round with swathes, for otherwise it would certainly fly to pieces. I often get a good laugh myself when these theologians that loom up so vast in their own eyes begin speaking in their slovenly and barbarous idiom and jabber so that no one except a jabberer can understand them, reaching a pitch—"highest acumen" they call it—

whereto the vulgar cannot climb. For they affirm that it suits not with the dignity of sacred discourse to be forced to obey the rules of grammarians. O marvellous prerogative of theologians, if to speak incorrectly is reserved to them alone! When the fact is that they share the distinction with most tinkers! Lastly, they consider themselves as next-door neighbors to the gods when they are addressed as "Our Masters," with almost religious reverence, in which title they fancy there lies such virtue as was in the "ineffable Four Letters" of the Hebrews. And going a little further, they say it is a sacrilege ever to write MAGISTER NOSTER except in capital letters; and if a person should happen to say *noster magister*, he has destroyed at one stroke all the majesty of the theological order.

[30] Coming nearest to these in felicity are the men who generally call themselves "the religious" and "monks"—utterly false names both, since most of them keep as far away as they can from religion and no people are more in evidence in every sort of place. But I do not see how anything could be more dismal than these monks if I did not succor them in many ways. For though people as a whole so detest this race of men that meeting one by accident is supposed to be bad luck, yet they flatter themselves to the queen's taste. For one thing, they reckon it the highest degree of piety to have no contact with literature, and hence they see to it that they do not know how to read. For another, when with asinine voices they bray out in church those psalms they have learned, by rote rather than by heart, they are convinced that they are anointing God's ears with the blandest of oil. Some of them make a good profit from their dirtiness and men-

dicancy, collecting their food from door to door with importunate bellowing; nay, there is not an inn, public conveyance, or ship where they do not intrude, to the great disadvantage of the other common beggars. Yet according to their account, by their very dirtiness, ignorance, want of manners, and insolence, these delightful fellows are representing to us the lives of the apostles.

What is funnier than to find that they do everything by rule, employing, as it were, the methods of mathematics; and to slip up is a great crime. There must be just so many knots for each shoe and the shoe-string must be of a certain color; the habit must be decked with just so much trimming; the girdle must be of a certain material and the width of so many straws; the cowl of a certain shape and a certain number of bushels in capacity; the hair so many fingers long; and one must sleep just so many hours. Who does not see that all this equality is really very unequal, in view of the great diversity of bodies and temperaments? Yet on the basis of such details they hold other people as mere nutshells. What is more, the members of one order, amid all their professions of apostolic charity, will turn and condemn the members of some other, making an admirable hubbub over the way their habit is belted or the slightly darker color of it. Among the monks you will see some so rigorously pious that they will wear no outer garment unless it be of Cilician goat's hair, while their inner garment is of Milesian wool; some others, on the contrary, are linen on the outside, but still wool underneath. Members of certain orders start back from the mere touch of a piece of money as if it were aconite. They do not, however, withdraw from the touch of a glass of wine, or of a woman. In short, all orders take remarkable care that nothing in their way of life shall be consistent; nor is it so much their concern to be like Christ as to be unlike each other. Thus a great part of their felicity derives from their various names. Those of one order delight to call themselves Cordeliers, but among them some are Coletes, some Minors, some Minims, some Crutched. Again, there are the Benedictines and the Bernardines; the Bridgetines and the Augustinians; the Williamists and the Jacobines; as if it were not enough to be called Christians.

The greater number of them work so hard at their ceremonies and at maintaining the minutiae of tradition that they deem one heaven hardly a suitable reward for their labors; never recalling that the time will come when, with all these things held of no account, Christ will demand a reckoning of that which He has prescribed, namely, charity. One friar will then show a paunch which has been padded out with every kind of fish; another will spill out a hundred bushels of hymns. Another will count off so many myriads of fasts, and will lay the blame for his almost bursting belly upon his having always broken his fasts by a single dinner. Another will point to a pile of ceremonies so big that seven ships could scarcely carry it. Another will boast that for sixty years he never touched money, except when his fingers were protected by two pairs of gloves. Another will wear a cowl so dirty and greasy that no sailor would deign to put it on. Another will celebrate the fact that for more than fifty-five years he lived the life of a sponge, always fastened to one spot. Another will show a voice grown hoarse with assiduous chanting; another, a lethargy contracted by living alone; another, a tongue grown dumb under his vow of silence. But Christ, interrupting their boasts, which otherwise would go on endlessly, will say: "Whence comes this new race of Jews? I recognize one commandment which is truly mine, and of that I hear nothing. Of old in the sight of all men and using no device of parable I promised the inheritance of my Father, not to cowls, orisons, or fasts, but to works of charity. Nor do I acknowledge those who acknowledge too well their own good works; let those that wish to seem holier than myself dwell, if they like, in those six hundred heavens of Basilides, or let them command a new heaven to be built for themselves by the very ones whose petty traditions they have preferred above my commandments." When they shall hear these words and shall see common sailors and teamsters preferred above them, with what faces, think you, will they look wistfully on each other! Yet meanwhile, with some assistance from me, they are happy in their good hope.

Yet nobody dares quite to scorn these people, though they are secluded from the life of the state; and least of all dares one scorn the mendicants, because they get hold of everybody's secrets by means of what they call confessions. To be sure, they account it a crime to publish these, except as it may happen, when they are in drink, that they wish to have some fun telling good stories, and will divulge a matter by hints, but suppressing, of course, the names. If anyone affronts these wasps, they will take suitable revenge in public sermons, and point out their enemy by indirect expressions so cunningly that no one will misunderstand unless he understands nothing. Nor will they make an end of barking until you throw a sop into their mouths.

[31] Tell me, what comic actor or mountebank would you rather watch than these monks rhetoricizing in their sermons, droll in every aspect, but neatly exemplifying all the lore which rhetoricians have handed down concerning the art of speaking. Good Lord! How they gesticulate, how aptly they modulate the voice, how they intone, throw themselves about, suddenly put on a new face, and confuse all things by their bawling! And this art of speaking is passed on traditionally from monk to brother monk as if it were a great craft and mystery. It is not lawful for me to know it, but I shall proceed with a few conjectures. They commence with an invocation, a trick which they have borrowed from the poets. Next, if they are to speak of charity, say, they begin their exordium with the river Nile in Egypt. Or if they are to expound the mystery of the Cross, they very happily take a start from Baal, the Babylonian snake-god. If they are to discuss fasting, they set out from the twelve signs of the Zodiac; or if they are to speak on faith, they make a few preliminary remarks on squaring the circle.

I have heard of a certain notable fool—there I go again! I meant to say scholar—who was about to explain the mystery of the Holy Trinity before a very distinguished audience. In order that he might at once make a display of his uncommon learning and give special satisfaction to the divines who were listening, he entered upon his matter in a completely new way—that is, from letters, syllables, and words; then from the agreement of noun and verb, of adjective and noun; while everybody was lost in wonder and some were murmuring to themselves that phrase from Horace, "What is all this stink about?" However, he drew out this observation, that in the elements of grammar he could show a symbol of the Holy Trinity, set forth so plainly that no mathematician could diagram it more clearly in the sand. And this superlative divine had so sweated and toiled on this sermon for the previous eight months that today he is as blind as a mole, all the sharpness of his sight having been exhausted, I fancy, to give edge to his wit. But the man does not begrudge his blindness, reckoning it a small price for the purchase of so much glory.

I heard another, a man of eighty years, and such a theologian that you would have thought Scotus reborn in his person. He was to explain the mystery of the name Jesus, and he showed with admirable subtlety that in the letters of the name was hidden everything that could be said about Him. The circumstance that the name is inflected in but three cases gives us a plain symbol of the threefold nature of God. Then the fact that in one case the name Jesus ends with s, in the second case it ends with m, and in the third with u lies an ineffable mystery, to wit, the three letters show that He is the *s*um, the *m*iddle, and the *u*ltimate. There remained a still more abstruse mystery in these letters treated mathematically; he divided the name Jesus into two equal parts in such a way that a fifth of it (the letter s) was left in the middle; then he pointed out that this letter among the Hebrews is שׁ, which they call *Schin*, or *Sin;* and that "sin" in the Scottish tongue, as he recalled, means *peccatum*. And from this he was able to declare in the sight of all men that it is Jesus who takes away the sin of the world! All his gaping hearers, and especially the theologues, were so struck with admiration of this new approach to the subject that what happened to Niobe came near to overtaking them;

though for my own part I came still nearer to imitating that shoddy Priapus who to his own great hurt witnessed the nocturnal rites of Canidia and Sagana. And with reason; for when did the Greek Demosthenes or the Roman Cicero ever cook up a rhetorical insinuation like that? They held that an introduction was faulty if it began too far from the matter itself, which, in fact, is the very way of beginning used by swineherds, who have mere nature for their guide. But these learned preachers consider that their preamble, for so they call it, will be eminently rhetorical only so far as it has no bearing upon the rest of the argument, to the end that the admiring auditor may murmur to himself, "Now what is he getting at?"

As a third step, by way of a substitute for a narration, they explain some bit from a Gospel, but hastily and by the way, as it were, when in fact it is the one thing they ought to drive home. For the fourth part, assuming a new character, they thresh over some question of divinity, relating, many times, to nothing on earth or in heaven; but such they suppose peculiarly to belong to their art. Here they rise to the height of theological majesty, sounding in the ears of the audience those august titles of Illustrious Doctor, Subtle Doctor, Supersubtle Doctor, Seraphic Doctor, Holy Doctor, Invincible Doctor. Then they bandy about, before an uneducated crowd, their syllogisms, majors, minors, conclusions, corollaries, conversions, and such bloodless and more than scholastic pedantry. There remains the fifth act, in which the proper thing is to exhibit the highest artistry. Here they bring in some silly and popular story drawn, I judge, from the *Speculum Historiale* or *Gesta Romanorum*, and interpret it allegorically, tropologically, and anagogically. And in this fashion they complete their chimera, one which Horace could not even approach when he wrote, *Humano capite*, etc.

But they have heard from some authorities, I know not which ones, that the beginning of a speech should be calm and not at all loud. Hence they start speaking their exordium in such a tone that they cannot hear their own voice, as if it did some good to speak what no one can catch. They have also been given to understand that to move the emotions one should use exclamations and a loud voice. Hence, although otherwise they have been going along with voice lowered, they now and then raise their voice on a sudden, with a furious roar, even when there is no occasion. You would swear that the man needed a dose of ipecac, except that the way he howls nothing would help him. Furthermore, because they have heard that as the sermon proceeds it should become more fervent, you notice that in scattered passages, no matter how the opening sections have been delivered, they employ a marvellous vehemency of voice, even when the subject-matter at those points is commonplace; and so at length they come to a close in a manner to make you think they are out of breath.

Lastly, they have learned that among the rhetoricians something is said about laughter, and they are eager to arouse it, sprinkling a jest here and there. And O golden Aphrodite! so gracefully turned, so apropos, that you would have to cry, "The ass is at the lyre!" They also try a bit of satire, but they tickle rather than wound; nor are they ever more soothing than when they mean to give the appearance of speaking with the greatest freedom. One more thing: their action is such that you would swear they had learned it from strolling players, though they fall far short of their teachers. Still each is so like the other that no one can doubt that the preachers learned from the players, or else the players learned their rhetoric from the preachers. And yet our preachers meet with some— and here I get in my work—who, when they listen to them, judge that they are hearing an absolute Demosthenes or Cicero. Most of this sort are either merchants or women, whose ears only the preachers study to please, because the merchants, if they are stroked the right way, are wont to pass over a little dividend of booty from their ill-gotten goods; and as to the women, though for many reasons they befriend the order, it is principally because they are accustomed to weep on their shoulders if for any reason they are at outs with their husbands. And now I am sure you perceive how much is owed to me by this class of men, who with their ceremonials and silly pedantries and bawling exercise a kind of despotism over mortal men, and believe themselves to be Pauls and Anthonies.

[32] In truth I am glad to get away from these actors and dissemblers, who are as ungrateful for my benefits as they are false in their pretensions to piety. And at this point it pleases me to touch upon kings and nobles of the court, by whom I am worshipped sincerely and, as becomes gentlemen, frankly. And indeed, if they had so much as half an ounce of sound wisdom, what life were more dismal than theirs or more to be avoided? For let a person weigh in his mind how heavy a burden rests on the shoulders of anyone wishing to act the true prince, and he will not conclude that sovereignty is a thing worth

using perjury and parricide to gain. He will consider that one who grasps the helm of great affairs must further the public, not his private, interest and give his mind to nothing except as it concerns the general good; he must not deviate a finger's breadth from the laws of which he is author and executor; he must himself be warrant for the integrity of all officials and magistrates; he is one person who is exposed to all eyes, and like a favorable star he has power, by the good influence of his conduct, to bring salvation in human affairs; or like a fatal comet he may bring destruction in his train. The vices of other men are not so deeply felt or so widely communicated. A prince is in such a position that if he lapses ever so slightly from honesty, straightway a dangerous and vital infection spreads to many people. Then the lot of princes brings with it a host of things which tend to lead them from righteousness, such as pleasure, liberty, adulation, and excess; so that he must endeavor more earnestly and watch more vigilantly lest, beguiled by these, he fail of his duty. Finally, to say nothing of treasons, hatreds, and other perils or dreads, there stands above his own crown that true King who will call him to account for even the least of his trespasses; and the accounting will be the more severe as the empire he ruled was the more mighty. I say that if the prince weighed these things, and many more like them, within himself—and he would do so, were he wise—I am afraid he could neither sleep nor eat in any joy.

But as it is, with my assistance, kings leave all these concerns to the gods, take care of themselves nicely, and grant no hearing to anyone unless he knows how to speak pleasant things, because solicitude must not get a foothold in their minds. They believe they have played the part of a sovereign to the hilt if they diligently go hunting, feed some fine horses, sell dignities and offices at a profit to themselves, and daily devise new measures by which to drain away the wealth of citizens and sweep it into their own exchequer. All this, of course, is done in due form, under new-found names, so that even when most unjust it shall carry some appearance of equity; and they take care to add a little sweetening so that in any event they may secure for themselves the hearts of the people. Fashion me now a man such as princes commonly are, a man ignorant of the laws, almost an enemy of the public welfare, intent upon private gain, addicted to pleasure, a hater of learning, a hater, too, of liberty and truth, thinking about anything except the safety of the state, and measuring all things by his own desire and profit. Then put on him a golden chain, symbolizing the union of all virtues linked together; set on him a crown adorned with gems, which is to remind him that he ought to surpass others in every heroic quality. In addition, give him a scepter, emblem of justice and of a heart in no way corrupted, and finally a scarlet robe, badge of a certain eminent love for the realm. If a prince really laid his own life alongside these symbols, I believe he would have the grace to be ashamed of his finery. He would be afraid some nosy satirist might turn the whole spectacle, suited as it is for high tragedy, into laughter and derision.

Now what shall I say about the noble courtiers? Though nothing is more venal, more servile, more witless, or more contemptible than most of them, yet they desire to seem the foremost of created things. Here is one point, however, in which they are as modest as one could

wish: they are satisfied to carry about on their bodies
gold, gems, scarlet, and the other insignia of wisdom and
the virtues, but the reality of these they leave for the use
of others. They find themselves abundantly happy in
being allowed to speak of the king as "our master," in
having learned how to turn a compliment in three words,
and in knowing how to repeat on occasion those cour-
teous titles of Your Grace, Your Lordship, and Your
Majesty; in having cast off shame beyond other men, and
in flattering handsomely. For these are the arts which
truly become the nobleman and courtier. For the rest, if
you look more closely at their whole way of life, you are
sure to find them "mere Phaeacians, suitors of Penelope,
and"—you know the rest of the verse, which Echo can
give you better than I. They sleep until noon, when a
hired chaplain comes to their bedside and swiftly runs
through matins before they are half up. Then to break-
fast, which is barely got through when dinner-time comes
along. After dinner come dice, checkers, cards, jesters,
fools, whores, dalliance, and horse-play. Meanwhile there
must be a round or two of drinks. Then back to supper,
with toasts after it—not just a toast, by Jove! And in this
fashion do their hours, days, months, years, and lives
glide away with no boredom. For myself it is as good as a
hearty meal to watch these high-flyers, observing how
every one of the ladies will think herself nearer to gods
the longer train she trails; while one of the noblemen will
shove past another by using his elbow, in order that he
may seem to stand a little closer to Jove; and each is the
more pleased with himself the heavier chain he can carry
about on his neck, as if he were showing off his strength
rather than his wealth.

BISHOPS AND CARDINALS

[33] Our popes, cardinals, and bishops for some time now have earnestly copied the state and practice of princes, and come near to beating them at their own game. Let a bishop but consider what his alb, the white emblem of sincerity, should teach him, namely, a life in every way blameless; and what is signified on his part by the two-horned miter, the two peaks bound by the same knot—I suppose it is a perfect knowledge of the Old and New Testaments; what is meant by covering his hands with gloves, a clean administration of the sacrament and one unsullied by any taint of human concerns; what the crozier symbolizes, most watchful care of the flock put under his charge; what is indicated by the cross that is carried before him, to wit, a victory over all carnal affections. If he would contemplate these and other lessons of the sort, I say, would he not lead a sad and troubled life? But as it is, they do well enough by way of feeding themselves; as for the other, the care of the sheep, they delegate that to Christ himself, or else refer it to their suffragans, as they call them, or other deputies. Nor do they keep in mind the name they bear, or what the word "bishop" means—labor, vigilance, solicitude. Yet in raking in moneys they truly play the bishop, overseeing everything—and overlooking nothing.

In a similar way the cardinals, if they considered the fact that they have succeeded to the places of the apostles, would see that the same works are required of them as were performed by their predecessors; that they are not lords, but stewards, of spiritual things, and that shortly they are to render an exact account of what they hold in trust. Yes, let them too philosophize a bit concerning their vestments, and question themselves in this fashion:

"What does the whiteness of this upper garment mean? Is it not a notable and singular purity of heart? What the crimson lower garment? Is it not a burning love of God? What, again, that outer robe flowing down in broad folds and spreading over the mule of his Exalted Reverence, though it would suffice to cover a camel? Is it not charity ample enough to embrace all men in its helpfulness, by way of teaching, exhorting, chastising, admonishing, ending wars, resisting wicked princes, and freely spending blood—not money alone—for the flock of Christ? And wherefore all this money, anyway, for those who hold the places of the needy apostles?" If they would weigh these things, I repeat, they would not be so ambitious for the post, and would willingly give it up, or at least they would lead a toilsome and watchful life of the sort lived by those ancient apostles.

As to these Supreme Pontiffs who take the place of Christ, if they tried to emulate His life, I mean His poverty, labors, teaching, cross, and contempt for safety, if even they thought upon the title of Pope—that is, Father—or the addition "Most Holy," who on earth would be more afflicted? Who would purchase that seat at the price of every resource and effort? Or who defend it, when purchased, by the sword, by poison, or by anything else? Were wisdom to descend upon them, how it would inconvenience them! Wisdom, did I say? Nay, even a grain of salt would do it—a grain of that salt which is spoken of by Christ. It would lose them all that wealth and honor, all those possessions, triumphal progresses, offices, dispensations, tributes, and indulgences; it would lose them so many horses, mules, and retainers; so many pleasures. (See how I have comprehended in a few words

many marketsful, a great harvest, a wide ocean, of goods!)
In place of these it would bring vigils, fasts, tears, prayers,
sermons, studies, sighs, and a thousand troublesome tasks
of the sort. Nor should we pass over the circumstance that
all those copyists and notaries would be in want, as would
all those advocates, promoters, secretaries, muleteers,
grooms, bankers, and pimps—I was about to add something more tender, though rougher, I am afraid, on the
ears. In short, that great host of men which burdens—I
beg your pardon, I mean adorns—the Roman See would
beg for their bread. This would be inhuman and down-
right abominable, and, what is more accursed, those very
princes of the church and true lights of the world would
themselves be reduced to a staff and a wallet.

As it is now, what labor turns up to be done they hand
over to Peter and Paul, who have leisure for it. But the
splendor and the pleasure they take care of personally.
And so it comes about—by my doing, remember—that
scarcely any kind of men live more softly or less oppressed
with care; believing that they are amply acceptable to
Christ if with a mystical and almost theatrical finery,
with ceremonies, and with those titles of Beatitude and
Reverence and Holiness, along with blessing and cursing,
they perform the office of bishops. To work miracles is
primitive and old-fashioned, hardly suited to our times;
to instruct the people is irksome; to interpret the Holy
Scriptures is pedantry; to pray is otiose; to shed tears is
distressing and womanish; to live in poverty is sordid; to
be beaten in war is dishonorable and less than worthy of
one who will hardly admit kings, however great, to kiss
his sacred foot; and finally, to die is unpleasant, to die on
the cross a disgrace.

There remain only those weapons and sweet benedictions of which Paul speaks, and the popes are generous enough with these: interdictions, excommunications, re-excommunications, anathematizations, pictured damnations, and the terrific lightning-bolt of the bull, which by its mere flicker sinks the souls of men below the floor of hell. And these most holy fathers in Christ, and vicars of Christ, launch it against no one with more spirit than against those who, at the instigation of the devil, try to impair or to subtract from the patrimony of Peter. Although this saying of Peter's stands in the Gospel, "We have left all and followed Thee," yet they give the name of his patrimony to lands, towns, tribute, imposts, and moneys. On behalf of these things, inflamed by zeal for Christ, they fight with fire and sword, not without shedding of Christian blood; and then they believe they have defended the bride of Christ in apostolic fashion, having scattered what they are pleased to designate as "her enemies." As if the church had any enemies more pestilential than impious pontiffs who by their silence allow Christ to be forgotten, who enchain Him by mercenary rules, adulterate His teaching by forced interpretations, and crucify Him afresh by their scandalous life!

Now the Christian church was founded on blood, strengthened by blood, and augmented by blood; yet nowadays they carry on Christ's cause by the sword just as if He who defends His own by His own means had perished. And although war is so cruel a business that it befits beasts and not men, so frantic that poets feign it is sent with evil purpose by the Furies, so pestilential that it brings with it a general blight upon morals, so iniquitous that it is usually conducted by the worst bandits, so impious that it has no accord with Christ, yet our popes, neglecting all their other concerns, make it their only task. Here you will see feeble old men assuming the strength of youth, not shocked by the expense or tired out by the labor, not at all discouraged, if only they may upset laws, religion, peace, and all humane usages, and turn them heels over head. Learned sycophants will be ofund who will give to this manifest madness the names of zeal, piety, and fortitude, devising a way whereby it is possible for a man to whip out his sword, stick it into the guts of his brother, and nonetheless dwell in that supreme charity which, according to Christ's precept, a Christian owes to his neighbor. Here I am at a loss as to whether certain bishops of the Germans furnished the popes the model for all this or took it from them. These bishops personally acted as colonels, laying by their garb, forgetting about benedictions and other such formalities, as though they esteemed it cowardly and lacking in decorum for a bishop to return his soul to God from any place but a battlefield.

Then the mob of priests, forsooth, consider it a sacrilege to fall short of their prelates in holiness. O brave! They war on behalf of their right to tithe in the best military manner, with swords, darts, stones, and force of arms. How keen-sighted they are, to elicit from the writings of the ancients something by which they can terrify the poor people and convince them that they owe more than their just tithes! Of course it does not occur to them that many things may be read in many scriptures touching the duty which they, on their side, should discharge as a debt to the people. Nor does their shaven crown in the least remind them that a priest ought to be free from all worldly desires and ought to set his mind upon nothing but heavenly things. These amiable men, on the contrary, say that they have well cleared themselves of their obligations if they somehow mutter those little prayers which, so help me, make me wonder whether any God hears or understands them, since the priests themselves barely hear them and do not understand them, even while they echo them with their mouths. But the priests have this much in common with the profane, that all alike watch for the harvest of profits, nor is a single one of them ignorant of the laws on this subject. Also, if there is any load to be borne, they cast it prudently on the shoulders of someone else, and thus one will shift it to another as men bandy a ball from hand to hand. As lay princes also entrust to ministers some parts of the ruling of their realm, and a minister turns over his share to some other minister, just so do priests, by reason of modesty, leave all pursuit of piety to the common folk; the folk cast it back on those whom they call "ecclesiastics," as if they themselves had no traffic whatever with the church and their baptismal vows had not the slightest effect. The priests, in turn, that call themselves "secular," as if admitted to the world, not to Christ, roll this burden off upon the regulars; the regulars put it upon the monks; the monks that have more liberty upon those that are stricter, and both together upon the mendicants; the mendicants upon the Carthusians, among whom, and nowhere else, piety lies hidden—and so lies that it is hardly permissible to find it out. Likewise the popes, so very diligent in reaping the pecuniary harvest, relegate their surplus of apostolic labors to the bishops; the bishops relegate them to the pastors, the pastors to the vicars, the vicars to the mendicant friars. These, however, push the care of the sheep back upon those who take the wool.

[34] But it is no part of my plan to canvass the lives of pontiffs and priests, for fear I should seem to compose a satire rather than pronounce a eulogy. And let no one think that good princes are taxed when I praise bad ones. But I have touched on these topics briefly in order to make clear to everyone that no mortal man can live happily unless he has been admitted to my mysteries and possesses my favor. For how else could it be, when Fortune herself, the directrix of human affairs, is so thoroughly of a mind with me that she always has been most hostile to the wise? But she brings all her gifts to fools, even while they are asleep. Have you not heard of one Timotheus who had a nickname and a proverb about him, "Fish came to his net when he was asleep." Again, there is the saying, "The owl flies." On the other hand, there are the proverbs that fit the wise: "He was born in the fourth month," and "He has the horse of Seius," and "gold of Toulouse." But I give up proverbializing, for fear I shall seem to have rifled the compilations of my good friend Erasmus.

To my subject, then. Fortune loves those who are less than discreet, she loves the rasher sort, and the ones who are fond of that saying, "The die is cast." But wisdom makes men meticulous, which is why you commonly see that the traffic of wise men is with poverty, hunger, and smoke; you see them living neglected, inglorious, and disliked. You see my fools abounding in money, holding the helms of states, in brief, flourishing every way. For if we esteem it a blessing to please princes and to mingle with such favorites of mine, these gods decked with gems, what is less to the purpose than wisdom? In the eyes of that rank of men, what, indeed, is more damning? If wealth is to be gathered, how much money would a merchant make if, running after wisdom, he should boggle at perjury, should blush to be taken in a lie, should in the least suffer from those inconvenient scruples of the wise touching theft and the taking of usury? Then if anyone sets his heart upon ecclesiastical honors and wealth, an ass or a buffalo will attain to them sooner than a wise man. If you are inclined to a certain sort of pleasure, the girls, a very important part of the human comedy, have given their hearts away to fools; they startle at a wise man and run from him, as from a scorpion. Lastly, whoever makes preparations to live a little more gaily and jovially will first of all shut the wise man out, and will prefer to let in any other animal. Wherever you circulate, in short, among popes, princes, judges, magistrates, friends, enemies, the great, or the humble, everything is done by cash in hand; and as the wise have contempt for cash, it carefully maintains the custom of avoiding them.

[35] Although there is no bound to my praises, or end of them, yet it is necessary that my oration shall have an end—sometime. And so I shall leave off speaking—but if first I shall show briefly that there have been great authors who have illustrated me by their writings, and as much by their goings-on, then perchance I shall not seem to have foolishly pleased only myself; and the lawyers cannot slander me by saying that "nothing is alleged." Hence, following their example, I allege my proofs, to wit, nothing to the point.

In the first place, all men agree with that familiar maxim, "If you don't have a thing, simulate it." And right along that line is the verse we teach to children, "To pretend to be a fool is sometimes the highest wisdom." You can figure for yourselves the great value of folly when the mere imitation of it, or pretense to it, is so highly esteemed by learned men. But much more frankly does that fat and sleek hog from the sty of Epicurus bid us "to mix in folly with our counsels"; although he rather discourteously puts in *brevem* ("a *little* folly"). Elsewhere he says, "It is sweet to play the fool in season." And in another passage he had rather "be giddy and taken for a dolt, than be wise and fret." Now Telemachus, in Homer, though the poet praises him every way he can, is now and then called "silly"; and the tragic dramatists usually speak of boys and youths with this same epithet, as if it were a lucky one. What does that revered poem, the *Iliad*, contain, if not the quarrels of foolish kings and peoples? Then too, how absolute is that commendation of Cicero's, "Everything is full of fools." Who has not learned that in proportion as a good is more widespread it is greater?

Perhaps among Christians the authority of these writers is weak. We shall also prop up our commendations, if you please, with the testimony of the Holy Scriptures, if only at the beginning, as learned writers customarily do, we display a permit from the theologians for what we are about to utter, so that they will wish us godspeed. Then, since we undertake a difficult task, and probably it would be unfair to call upon the Muses again for such a long journey from Helicon to here—especially since the business is out of their line—I think it more suitable while I play the divine and tread among thorns to beg that the soul of Scotus, itself more prickly than a porcupine or hedgehog, shall come from his beloved Sorbonne and dwell in my breast for a season; and very soon it shall go back whither it pleases, or to the dogs. Would that it were possible to put on another face and come rigged out as a divine, also! Indeed, as it is, I fear it: someone will lay against me the charge of theft, as if I had secretly plundered the portfolios of Our Masters, because I have so much theological property in my possession. Yet really it should not seem strange that I have picked up a little, since for a long time I have been in closest contact with the divines. You recall that the pinchbeck god Priapus learned and retained some Greek words, merely by hearing his master read. The cock in Lucian, by long association with men, became skilled in human speech.

Now to the business, under favorable auguries. Ecclesiastes has written in his first chapter: "The number of fools is infinite." When he terms the number infinite, does he not seem to embrace mortals generally, unless for a few—and I do not know that anyone has ever had the luck to see them. But Jeremiah testifies more ingenuously in his tenth chapter, saying, "Every man is made foolish by his own wisdom." He attributes wisdom to God alone, leaving folly as the portion of all men. And again, a little earlier: "Let not man glory in his wisdom." Why do you not wish man to glory in his wisdom, excellent Jeremiah? For the simple reason, he would of course answer, that he has no wisdom. But I return to Ecclesiastes. Thus when he writes, "Vanity of vanities, all is vanity," what else do you think he means but that, just as I have told you, human life is nothing but a sport of folly? And indeed he adds an affirmative vote to the sentiment of Cicero, over whose great name is set down, as I mentioned just now,

"Everything is full of fools." Again, when the wise Ecclesiasticus said that "the fool is changed as the moon," but that "the wise man is as fixed as the sun," what did he intend to show except that the whole human race is foolish, and the attribute of wisdom is meet for God alone? For interpreters always read "moon" as human nature, and "sun," the source of all light, as God. In agreement with this we find Christ in the Gospels forbids that anyone should be called good but one, and that is God. If a man who is not wise, then, is a fool, and whoever is good is *ipso facto* wise, in accordance with Stoic writers, it is a necessary conclusion that folly comprehends all men. Again Solomon, Chapter 15: "A fool," he says, "delights in his folly," that is, he clearly acknowledges that without folly nothing in life is sweet. That other text tends to the same effect: "He that increaseth knowledge increaseth sorrow, and in much wisdom is much grief." And does not the famous Preacher openly confess the same in Chapter 7: "The heart of the wise is where sadness is, but the heart of fools follows mirth." By this you see that he held it not enough to have learned wisdom if you have not also added a knowledge of me. But if you put little faith in me, take the words he wrote in Chapter 1: "I gave my heart to know wisdom, and to know madness and folly." In this passage it is to be noted that the advantage rests with folly, since he put it in the last place. Ecclesiastes wrote that, and you know the ecclesiastical order is for him that is first in dignity to get the last place, observing in this, at least, the precept of the Gospels.

But that folly is more excellent than wisdom, Ecclesiasticus, whoever he was, makes as clear as crystal in Chapter 44—whose words, so help me, I shall not quote until you accord my opening a suitable response, just the way, in Plato, the fellows do who dispute with Socrates. Now, is it more suitable to hide carefully away things that are rare and precious, or things that are vulgar and cheap? . . . Why don't you say something? . . . Well, even if you are dissembling, the Greek proverb will answer for you: "Buckets are left in doorways." (If any impious fellow is inclined to sniff at this saying, let him know that Aristotle, the god of Our Masters, reports it.) But which of you is such a fool as to leave gems and gold lying in the street? . . . I think none, so help me. You put them in the most hidden recesses; and that is not enough, in the most secret corners of your best guarded chests. But you throw dirt outdoors. Ergo, if what is more precious is hidden up, and what is more base is put out in the open, is it not clear that wisdom, which Ecclesiasticus forbids us to hide, is worth less than folly, which he bids us conceal? Now you can have his own words: "Better is the man that hideth his folly than he that hideth his wisdom." Or what about the passage wherein Holy Writ attributes honesty of soul to the fool, while the wise man all the while thinks there is no one like himself? For so I understand what Ecclesiastes wrote in Chapter 10: "A fool walking by the way, being a fool, esteems all men as fools." And is not that a remarkable kind of honesty, to hold all equal with oneself, and in a world where everybody thinks of himself in a complimentary way, to share one's praises with all? For that cause the great King Solomon was not ashamed of the name, when he said in Chapter 30, "I am the most foolish of men."

Paul, the great teacher of the Gentiles, writing to the Corinthians, freely owned to the name: "I speak as a fool," he said; "I am more." This is as if it were a disgraceful thing to be outdone in folly. But now some Greeklings, grackle-like, will break in upon me with their clamor; they are zealous to peck at modern theologians, quite as if they were pecking out the eyes of crows; while they spread their own annotations like smoke over the commentary of others. In the register of this band my Erasmus (whom I often mention *honoris causa*) is listed as *alpha*, or if not, then at least as *beta*. "O foolish citation," these Greeklings will say, "one worthy of Folly herself! The sense of the apostle is far different from what you dream it to be. For he did not intend by these words to have them believe him a greater fool than the rest. But when he had said, 'Are they ministers of Christ? So am I,' and had equalled himself to others in this respect, somewhat led into boasting he added as an emphatic correction, 'I am more,' meaning that he was not only equal to the other apostles in the ministry of the gospel, but was superior to them. And though he wished this to be received as true, yet for fear such an arrogant phrase would offend their ears, he guarded himself by the suggestion of folly—'I speak as a fool'—as if he would say that it is the privilege of fools that they alone may speak the truth without offense."

But whatever Paul thought when he wrote these words, I leave to them to dispute about. I follow the great, fat, dull, and generally approved theologians, with whom the large majority of learned men choose to err, by Jove, rather than to understand aright with these trilinguists. No one among the majority accounts these Greeklings as anything more than grackles, especially when a certain renowned divine, whose name I suppress out of prudence (for fear our grackles would constantly throw up at him that Greek gibe about the ass and the *Lyra*), by way of expounding in magisterial and theological fashion this passage, from the words, "I speak as a fool; I am more," began a new chapter in his book, and even—something that could not be done without the keenest logic—began a new section. He interpreted it in this fashion—for I shall give you his very words, in form as well as in substance: " 'I speak as a fool.' That is, if I seem to you a little foolish in making myself equal to those false apostles, I must seem more foolish in making myself superior to them." This same author, however, as if forgetting himself, a little later slips off into another interpretation.

[36] But why should I solicitously defend myself with the example of one man, when it is the lawful prerogative of divines to stretch heaven, that is, the Holy Scriptures, as they would stretch a piece of sheepskin? If we may place any credit in Jerome, master of five languages, even in Paul some words of Holy Scripture are in conflict, though in their context they seem not to conflict at all. Thus when, speaking to the Athenians, he went about to twist the inscription he had seen on an altar into an argument for the Christian faith, he omitted most of the words because they were against his purpose and picked out only four from the end, "to the Unknown God." These he altered, since the whole inscription read, "To the Gods of Asia, Europe, and Africa, to the Unknown Gods, and Foreign Gods." It must be by his example that our "sons of theologues" in these days will ordinarily accommodate to their own purpose four or five little words plucked out from here and there, even depraving the sense of them, if need be; although the words which precede and follow

these are nothing at all to the point or even go against it. Theologians do this with such felicitous effrontery that our lawyers oftentimes become jealous of them.

For to what length may they not go now, after this great divine—I almost let slip his name, but again I am afraid of the Greek proverb—has squeezed out of some words of Luke's a meaning precisely as congruent with the spirit of Christ as fire is with water. It is when the extreme trial was drawing near, a time when retainers and dependents usually make a special point of being with their patron, to organize for battle with what resources they may have at hand. Christ, acting to the end that He might remove from the minds of His followers all hope for a defence of that kind, questioned them as to whether anything needful had been lacking when He sent them forth quite unequipped for travelling, since He neither furnished shoes to protect their feet against thorns and stones nor gave them a wallet to provide against hunger. When they denied that anything was lacking, He went on: "But now, he that hath a bag, let him take it, and likewise a wallet; and he that hath not a sword, let him sell his coat and buy one." Since the entire teaching of Christ enforces nothing but meekness, patience, contempt of life, who does not clearly perceive the meaning of this passage? I take it that He purposed to disarm His ministers still more, so that not only neglecting shoes and wallet but throwing away their coat as well, they might, stripped and wholly disengaged, proceed to the work of the Gospel. They were to provide themselves with nothing but a sword—not the sword with which bandits and murderers attack, but the sword of the spirit, which penetrates into the secret places of the breast and at one stroke cuts off all earthly affections, so that the heart has place for no other passion than piety.

But observe, I pray, how this celebrated theologian wrested these words. He interpreted "sword" as "defense against persecution," and "bag" as "sufficient provision of supplies"; as if Christ, with His mind so changed that it now seemed He had sent out His exhorters less royally equipped than they should be, made a recantation of His former doctrine; or as if forgetting He had said they would be blessed when they were assailed by reproaches, by evil speaking, by punishments, and had forbidden them to resist evil because the meek are blessed; as if forgetting also that He had urged upon them the example of the sparrows and of lilies, and now was so unwilling they should go without a sword that he bade them buy one even by selling their coat, preferring that they should go naked rather than not girt round with a good blade. On top of this our theologue, you recall, intends that by the word "sword" is embraced whatever is necessary for repelling violence, and by the word "bag" is embraced whatever is necessary to support life. And so this interpreter of the divine mind leads forth the apostles equipped with lances, crossbows, slings, and muskets, for the task of preaching Christ crucified. He loads them with portmanteaus also, with hand-bags, and knapsacks—for fear it would be the rule, perchance, that they must always leave their inn without eating. Nor has it disturbed this interpreter that He who thus earnestly bade that a sword be purchased, soon after with a rebuke ordered the same weapon to be sheathed; or that no one has ever heard it told that the apostles used swords or shields against the violence of the heathen, though they would have used them if Christ had meant what the interpreter finds here.

It was another, whose name I omit out of respect, and not at all because it is a bad name, who made out of the tents which Habakkuk mentions—"the skins of the land of the Midians will be shaken"—the skin of St. Bartholomew, who was flayed. I myself lately. attended a theological discussion (as I frequently do); when someone asked what injunction there is in Holy Scripture bidding that heretics shall be wiped out by fire rather than confuted by argument, a certain severe old fellow whose haughtiness proclaimed the theologian replied with a good deal of animosity that the Apostle Paul laid down this rule when he said, "A man that is an heretic, after the first and second admonition reject," the word for "reject" being *devita*. And when he had thundered out these words again and again, and most of his hearers were wondering what had struck the man, he at length explained that the heretic was to be removed *de vita*, from life! Some burst out laughing, and yet there were others to whom this discovery seemed absolutely theological. Against the few who still raised voices in opposition the Tenedian lawyer (as the phrase is) and irrefragable commentator pursued the argument. "Take this point," he said. "It is written, 'Thou shalt not suffer a witch [*maleficum*] to live.' Every heretic is a witch [*maleficus* = bad, villainous]. Ergo," etc. Those present admired his powers of mind and went along with him, flat-footedly, in his reasoning. It did not come into anyone's head that this injunction applied only to sorcerers, enchanters, and magicians, whom the Hebrews in their tongue call *Mekaschephim*, which we translate as *malefici* or "witches."

For otherwise—using *maleficus* as above—it would be incumbent upon us to punish fornication and drunkenness by death.

But I am foolish to pursue these points, which are so numberless that all of them could not be contained in the books of Chrysippus or Didymus. At least I wish you to keep this in mind, that since things like that are permitted to theological masters, it is but fair to allow the same indulgence also to me (who am obviously but a pinchbeck divine), if I shall not make every quotation and citation with absolute exactness. Now at last I get back to Paul. "Suffer fools gladly," he says, speaking of himself; and again, "Receive me as a fool"; also, "I do not speak according to God, but as if in foolishness." Again, he says in another place, "We are fools for Christ's sake." From so great a writer you hear such great commendations of folly! What he does, in fact, is publicly to teach and enjoin this folly as a thing specially necessary and good for the town: "Let him that seems to be wise among you become a fool, that he may be wise!" And in Luke, the two disciples with whom Jesus joined company on the highway He called "fools." Nor do I know any reason why it should seem strange that Paul attributed a measure of folly even to God: "The foolishness of God," he said, "is wiser than men." To be sure, Origen in his interpretation objects that this foolishness can hardly be equivalent to the ordinary fancies of men; which last are indicated in that other passage: "The preaching of the Cross is to them that perish foolishness."

[37] Yet why am I so needlessly careful in going about to support these matters by all these proofs and witnesses when in the mystical psalms Christ himself, speaking to

the Father, says for all men to hear, "Thou knowest my foolishness"? Nor indeed is it without cause that fools are so vastly pleasing to God; the reason being, I suggest, that just as great princes look suspiciously on men who are too clever, and hate them—as Julius Caesar suspected and hated Brutus and Cassius while he did not fear drunken Antony at all, Nero was suspicious of Seneca, Dionysius of Plato—while on the other hand they take delight in duller and simpler souls; so Christ detests and condemns those wise men who rely on their own prudence. Paul witnesses to this very clearly when he says, "God has chosen the foolish things of the world," and when he says, "It has pleased God to save the world by foolishness," seeing that it could never be redeemed by wisdom. But God points this out clearly enough, when He cries through the mouth of the prophet, "I will destroy the wisdom of the wise, and I will reject the prudence of the prudent." And again, our Lord gave thanks that God had concealed the mystery of salvation from the wise, but had revealed it to babes, that is, to fools. For the Greek word for "babes" is νηπίοις, generally used as the opposite to σοφοῖς, "the wise." It tends to the same effect when in the Gospels He often attacks the scribes and Pharisees and doctors of the law, whereas He faithfully defends the ignorant multitude. For what is "Woe unto you, scribes and Pharisees" except "Woe unto you that are wise?" But He seems to find most potent delight in little children, women, and fishermen. And even in the class of brute creatures, those which are farthest from a foxlike cunning were best pleasing to Christ. He preferred to ride upon a donkey, though had He chosen He could have mounted the back of a lion without danger. And the

Holy Spirit descended in likeness of a dove, not of an eagle or a kite. Here and there in Holy Writ, furthermore, there is repeated mention of harts, fawns, and lambs. Add to this that Christ calls those who are destined to eternal life by the name "sheep"—and there is no other creature more foolish, as is witnessed by the proverbial phrase in Aristotle, "sheepish temperament," which he tells us was suggested by the stupidity of the animal and commonly used as a taunt against dull-witted and foolish men. And yet Christ avows himself as shepherd of this flock and even delights in the name of Lamb, as when John pointed Him out, "Behold the Lamb of God!" There is much use of this term also in the book of *Revelations*.

What do all these things cry out to us if not this, that mortal men, even the pious, are fools? And that Christ, in order to relieve the folly of mankind, though Himself "the wisdom of the Father," was willing in some manner to be made a fool when He took upon Himself the nature of a man and was found in fashion as a man? And likewise He was made "to be sin" that He might heal sinners. Nor did He wish to bring healing by any other means than by "the foolishness of the cross," and by weak and stupid apostles upon whom He carefully enjoined folly, dissuading them from wisdom, while He incited them by the example of children, lilies, mustard-seed, and sparrows— witless things and deficient in sense, living their lives by the guidance of nature with no art or anxious care. Beyond this, He forbade them to be troubled about what they should say before magistrates and He charged that they should not inquire into times and seasons; in a word, they should not trust to their own wisdom but wholly depend upon Him. To the same effect we learn that God, architect of the world, charged upon pain of death that men should not eat of the tree of knowledge, exactly as if knowledge is the bane of happiness. Likewise Paul specifically disavows knowledge as that which puffs up and works harm. St. Bernard is following him, I suppose, when he interprets that mountain whereon Lucifer established his headquarters as "the Mount of Knowledge."

It would seem, surely, that we ought not overlook this argument, that folly is so acceptable to the heavenly powers that forgiveness of its errors is assured, whereas nothing is forgiven to wisdom; whence it comes about that when the prudent pray for pardoning grace, though they were prudent enough when they sinned, they use the excuse and defense of having acted foolishly. For thus Aaron in the book of *Numbers*, if I recall aright, begged that the punishment of his sister might be remitted: "I beseech, my master, that you lay not this sin, which we have committed foolishly, to our charge." Thus also Saul asked from David pardon for his fault, saying, "For it is apparent that I have done foolishly." David himself, in turn, speaks fair to God: "But I pray, O Lord, that Thou mayst take away the iniquity of Thy servant, because I have done foolishly," as if he could not obtain grace by his request unless he pleaded folly and ignorance. But the point is proved still more cogently by the fact that Christ, when He prayed on the Cross for His enemies, "Father, forgive them," pleaded no other mitigation than ignorance, saying, "for they know not what they do." In like manner Paul wrote to Timothy: "But therefore I have obtained the mercy of God, because being ignorant I acted in unbelief." What is the meaning of "being

ignorant I acted" except "I acted foolishly, not ma-
liciously"? What is "But therefore I obtained the mercy
of God" except "I should not have obtained it except as
I was made more pardonable by the excuse of folly"?
The mystical psalmist—though I forgot to use the quotation in its proper place—supports me: "Remember not
the sins of my youth and my ignorances." You have
heard him making two excuses—youth, with which I am
always a present companion, and ignorance; and this
last in the plural number, so that we are to understand a
great flood of folly.

[38] But I should not further pursue that which is infinite; let me speak compendiously. The Christian religion on the whole seems to have a kinship with some
sort of folly, while it has no alliance whatever with wisdom. If you want proofs of this statement, observe first of
all how children, old people, women, and fools find
pleasure beyond other folk in holy and religious things,
and to that end are ever nearest the altars, led no doubt
solely by an impulse of nature. Then you will notice that
the original founders of religion, admirably laying hold of
pure simplicity, were the bitterest foes of literary learning.
Lastly, no fools seem to act more foolishly than do the
people whom zeal for Christian piety has got possession
of; for they pour out their wealth, they overlook wrongs,
allow themselves to be cheated, make no distinction between friends and enemies, shun pleasure, glut themselves with hunger, wakefulness, tears, toils, and reproaches; they disdain life and dearly prefer death; in
short, they seem to have grown utterly numb to ordinary
sensations, quite as if their souls lived elsewhere and not
in their bodies. What is this, forsooth, but to be mad?

Whereby we should find it less strange that the apostles appeared to be drunk with new wine, and that Paul, in the eyes of his judge, Festus, looked as if he had gone mad.

Come, now that I have "put on the lion's skin," I shall show this also, that the happiness of Christians, which they pursue with so much travail, is nothing else but a kind of madness and folly. Let these words give no offense; instead, keep your mind on the point. To begin with, Christians come near to agreeing with Platonists in this, that the soul is sunk and shackled by corporeal bonds, being so clogged by the grossness of the body that but little can it contemplate and enjoy things as they truly are. Hence Plato defined philosophy as "a study of death," because it leads the mind away from visible and bodily things, and certainly death does the same. And thus as long as the soul uses the bodily organs aright, so long it is called sane, but when with its bonds broken it attempts to make good its liberty, planning, as it were, escape from its prison, then it is called mad. If perchance this condition arises from sickness or a defect of some organ, then by common consent it is unmistakable insanity. Yet we see men of this sort predict future events, we see them understand languages and discourse which they have not previously known, and in general manifest something partaking of the divine. No doubt this happens because as the soul is a little more free from the taint of the body, it begins to exert its own native powers. I conceive the same to be the cause that something very similar is wont to happen with those who are near death in their sufferings. As if inspired, they speak things far above a common strain. Yet if such a thing results from zeal for religion, perhaps it is not the same sort of madness but so near to it that the greater part of mankind will judge it to be mere insanity, especially in view of the fact that only a handful of unimportant people out of the whole society of mortals thus differ completely from the rest in their way of life.

And so it ordinarily fares with men as it fared in Plato's myth, I gather, between those who admired shadows, still bound in the cave, and that one who broke away and, returning to the doorway, proclaimed that he had seen realities and that they who believed nothing existed except shadows were greatly deceived. Just as this wise man pitied and deplored the madness of those who were gripped by such an error, they, on their side, derided him as if he were raving, and cast him out. In like fashion the great masses of people admire what things are most corporeal and deem that such come near to being the only things they are. The religious, on the contrary, pay less attention to anything the more nearly it concerns the body, and they are wholly rapt away in the contemplation of things unseen. For the majority assign the leading rôle to riches and the next to bodily comforts, while they leave the lowliest for the soul, which most of them, however, believe does not exist, because it is not seen by the eye. In quite different fashion the religious with one accord direct their first endeavors toward God himself, the purest of all existences; next Him, toward that which yet comes as close as possible to Him, namely, the soul. They neglect the care of the body. They altogether disdain riches as mere nutshells, and turn their backs upon them. Or if they are forced to handle matters of the kind, they do so grudgingly and uneasily, having as if they did not have, possessing as if they did not possess.

THE PIOUS VS. THE WORLD

On particular points there are great degrees of difference between these two sorts of persons. In the first place, although all the senses have alliance with the body, certain of them are grosser, such as touch, hearing, sight, smell, taste, while certain ones are less closely tied up with the body, as the memory, intellect, and will. To whichever one the soul applies itself, that one grows strong. Forasmuch as every energy of the devout soul strives toward objects which are at farthest remove from the grosser senses, these grow numb, as it were, and stupefy; whence it comes that we hear about saints who have chanced to drink oil in place of wine. Among the passions and impulses of the mind, again, some have more connection with the physical body, as lust, love of food and sleep, anger, pride, envy. With these the pious are irreconcilably at war, while the multitude, on the other hand, consider that without them life does not exist. Then there are some feelings of a middle sort, merely natural, so to speak, such as love of one's father, affection for one's children, relatives, and friends; to these feelings the multitude pays considerable respect, but the pious endeavor to pluck them, too, out of their minds, except so far as, rising to the highest spiritual plane, they love a parent not as parent—for what did he beget but the body, and even that is owed to God as Father—but rather as a good man, one in whom is manifest the impress of that Supreme Mind which they call the *summum bonum* and beyond which, they assert, nothing is to be loved or sought for.

By the same rule they also measure all others of life's duties, and in general they either scorn that which is visible or make much less of it than of things invisible.

They say also that both body and spirit enter into the sacraments and into the very offices of piety; as in fasting, they do not account it of much worth if a person abstains from meats or from a meal, that which the vulgar esteem an absolute fast, unless at the same time he in some measure frees himself from passions, yielding less than he is wont to anger, less to pride; and then the spirit, weighed down less by the burden of the body, may climb upwards even to the partaking and enjoying of celestial bounties. In like manner, too, with the Eucharist, although it is not to be slighted, they say, merely because it is administered with ceremonies, yet of itself it is either of little profit or indeed harmful except so far as that which is spiritual is added to it—in a word, that which is represented under the visible symbols. For the death of Christ is so represented, and this it behooves mortal men to translate into the taming, extinguishing, and, as it were, burying of their carnal affections; that they may arise to a newness of life and be made one with Him, and one also with each other. Thus a devout man does, and such is his contemplation. The crowd, on the other hand, believes that the sacrament is no more than coming to the altar, as close as may be, hearing the noise of words, and watching the whole pageant of ceremonial details. Nor in this alone, which I set forth merely as an example, but in all of his life the pious man sincerely forsakes whatever has alliance with the body and is drawn to eternal, invisible, and spiritual objects.

[39] Wherefore, since there is so great contrariety between the pious and the vulgar, it comes about that each appears to the other to be mad—though in my opinion, to be sure, the word is more correctly applied to the pious

than to the others. This will become clearer if I briefly demonstrate, as I promised to do, that their *summum bonum* itself is no other than a kind of insanity. First, let us suppose that Plato was dreaming of something very like it when he wrote that "the madness of lovers is the happiest state of all." Now he who loves intensely no longer lives in himself but in whatever he loves, and the more he can depart from himself and enter into the other, the happier he is. And when a mind yearns toward travelling out of the body, and does not rightly use its own bodily organs, you doubtless, and with accuracy, call the state of it madness. Otherwise, what do they mean by those common phrases, "he is not at home," and "to come to yourself," and "he is himself again"? Furthermore, so far as the love is more perfect the madness is greater and more delightful. Of what sort, then, is that future life with those who dwell on high, toward which pious hearts aspire with such fervor? First the spirit, as conqueror and the more vital, will overmaster and absorb the body, and this it will do the more easily in that now it is in its own realm, so to speak, and also because already, during life, it has cleansed and lightened the body in preparation for this change. Then the spirit itself will be absorbed in marvellous wise by that supreme spirit, more potent than its infinity of parts. Thus the whole man will be outside of himself, nor will he be happy for any other reason than that, so placed outside of himself, he shall have some ineffable portion in that *summum bonum* which draws all things unto itself. And although this happiness arrives at its perfection only when souls, joined to their former bodies, shall be clothed with immortality, yet because the earthly life of pious folk is nothing but a contemplation and kind of shadowing of that other, they sometimes feel a foretaste and a glow of the reward to come. Although this is as but the least little drop in comparison with that flowing fountain of eternal happiness, yet it far surpasses any bodily pleasure, yes, even if all mortal delights were brought together into one. By so much does the spiritual excel over the corporeal, and the invisible over the visible. This surely is what the prophet has promised: "Eye hath not seen, nor ear heard, neither have entered into the heart of man the things which God hath prepared for them that love Him." And this truly is the portion of Folly, that "good part" which "shall not be taken away" by the transformation of life, but will be perfected.

Hence those who are permitted to have a foretaste of this—and it comes to but few—suffer something very like to madness. They say things that are not quite coherent, and this not in the ordinary way of men, but they make a sound without meaning, and suddenly they change the whole aspect of their faces; now cheerful, now downcast, they will weep, then laugh, and then sigh; in brief, they are truly outside themselves. When presently they return to themselves they say that they do not know where they have been, whether in the body or out of it, waking or sleeping; they do not remember what they have heard, seen, spoken, or done; and yet through a cloud, or as in a dream, they know one thing, that they were at their happiest while they were thus out of their wits. So they are sorry to come to themselves again and would prefer, of all good things, nothing but to be mad always with this madness. And this is a tiny little taste of that future happiness.

PERORATION

[40] But indeed I have long since forgotten myself and run out of bounds. If anything I have said shall seem too saucy or too glib, stop and think: 'tis Folly, and a woman, that has spoken. But of course you will also remember that Greek proverb, "Even a foolish man will often speak a word in season," unless, perhaps, you assume that this does not extend to women. I see that you are expecting a peroration, but you are just too foolish if you suppose that after I have poured out a hodgepodge of words like this I can recall anything that I have said. There is an old saying, "I hate a pot-companion with a memory." Here is a new one: "I hate a hearer that remembers anything."

And so farewell. . . . Applaud . . . live . . . drink . . . O most distinguished initiates of Folly!

COMMENTARY

Analysis

EFERENCE HAS BEEN MADE, IN THE INTRODUC-
tory essay, to the logical and rhetorical structure
of *The Praise of Folly*. The outline or brief below
will make clear this structure. The form used is
the traditional one drawn from analysis of the
classical oration. The main parts, in this form, are the
Exordium (designed to win attention and conciliate the
audience), the Narration (presenting reasons for speaking or the factual basis of the question, or both), the Partition (dividing the subject and indicating the main
topics to be pursued), the Confirmation, or Argument
(the main body of the speech), and the Peroration. Sometimes the Proposition, a statement and definition of the
subject, was made a separate part, but often it was
thought of as belonging with the Partition. The classical
form also allowed for one or more digressions, usually in
the Confirmation. It will be observed that in Section 31
of the eulogy, when Folly ridicules the preaching of the
friars, she goes over this same form of outline as it appears
in their sermons.

The brief shows logical relations and order of ideas. It
does not show the great variety of methods used by
Erasmus to introduce and to develop these ideas. His
transitions are worth special attention. Page-references
have been given for the main headings, so that a notion
may be gained of the proportion of time spent upon each
of the various topics. We find that Erasmus often develops

at great length what appears in the brief as a very minor point. One might say that he feels free to dwell upon whatever idea catches his fancy and stimulates his mind. Yet in well organized arguments, such as these are, a contention placed in a most subordinate position is the ultimate support of all placed above it. Thus when Erasmus expends several pages upon what appears in the brief as point XI C 6 h (2), "They [the preaching friars] use farfetched exordia," he is abundantly proving point h, "Their preaching is absurd," which in turn supports point 6, "The follies of monks make them happy," and this is one part of the ground covered by the main point, XI, "All people are followers of Folly." Incidentally, this eleventh main point, as its inclusive nature warrants, gives rise to the longest treatment of any—about one-fourth of the eulogy. Yet space is not the only criterion of importance. From the moment that Erasmus introduces his criticism of theologians (Section 28) to the beginning of the peroration there is a rising movement—a tightening of grasp and a deepening of essential seriousness. The movement is not unbroken. In order to maintain some consistency with the earlier part—and perhaps by way of "comic relief"—Erasmus gives the brief argument that "Fortune favors fools" (Section 34) and indulges in a certain amount of fooling in Section 35. But that the order of climax is well observed, and that the last argument (Sections 38-39), dealing with "Christian folly," is in the author's view the most important thing he has to say, one cannot well doubt.

The unequal allotment of space, however, makes it impossible to divide the declamation into sections, for purposes of reference, exactly according to the headings of the outline. The translator has divided it into forty sections of fairly equal length, numbered by Arabic numerals in brackets, and the division will be found to accord with important units of thought. Section-numbers are placed in the margin of the outline so as to indicate the relation of each section to the progress of the logical argument.

It is possible to discern, over and above the analysis as given, a three-fold division of the Confirmation, in which the headings would be: (I) *Folly is truly a goddess* (including all the present headings I-X); (II) *All people worship her* (heading XI); (III) *She is approved by poets, prophets, and deities* (headings XII-XIV). The first of these three divisions is the hardest to see as a unit; and it has been thought best not to attempt treating it (or the third one) as such in the present analysis. But that this tripartite scheme more or less definitely underlies the eulogy may well be argued.

[PROPOSITION: FOLLY DESERVES THE PRAISE OF ALL.]

Exordium (pp. 7-8)

[1]   I. Folly's mere appearance makes her welcome.
       II. Her garb is explained by her purpose.

Narration (pp. 8-9)

[2]   I. It is proper that Folly should praise herself.
        A. She knows herself best.
        B. To do so is more modest than hiring a publicity agent.
        C. One should praise one's self if no one else will do it.
        D. Orators have praised much worse subjects.
      II. Her speech will be extempore.

THE PRAISE OF FOLLY

Partition (pp. 9-11)

[3]   I. She will not define or divide herself.
     II. She is as you see her.
       A. She can be recognized even in those who try to hide her.
    III. [Digression] She will imitate modern rhetoricians and sprinkle in a few Greek words.

Confirmation (pp. 11-124)

[4]   I. Folly is great in her ancestry and birth. (pp. 11-12)
       A. She is the child of Plutus and Youth.
       B. Plutus, her father, is greatest of all gods.
       C. She was not born in wedlock.
     II. She is great in her birthplace and early care. (pp. 12-13)
       A. She was born in the Fortunate Isles.
       B. She was nursed by Drunkenness and Ignorance.
    III. She has distinguished assistants. (p. 13)
       A. She is attended by Drunkenness, Ignorance, Self-Love, Flattery, Forgetfulness, Laziness, Pleasure, Madness, Wantonness, Intemperance, and Sleep.
[5] IV. She has rightful claims to divinity. (pp. 13-22)
       A. She is divine in the greatness of her power.
         1. She is responsible for our birth.
[6]   2. She gives pleasure, the true principle of life.
           a. The young and the old are happiest.
           b. Her making the old into children again is the pleasantest of metamorphoses.
           c. She keeps people young.
[7]   3. She has power over the other gods.
[8]   B. Human happiness depends upon folly. (pp. 22-28)
         1. The attempt of reason to govern breaks down.
         2. Men get happiness from women, who are fools.

3. Conviviality depends upon folly for its power to please.

[9]   4. Friendship needs folly as an aid.

5. Marriage needs folly.

[10]   C. Folly's chief companion, Philautia, also brings happiness. (pp. 28-30)

1. A man must be satisfied with himself to have pleasure or to be tolerable to others.

2. Self-love makes possible all of one's accomplishments.

3. Self-love prevents shame and discontent.

[11] V. All great actions depend upon Folly and her companions. (pp. 30-35)

A. War depends upon folly.

1. It is foolish in its whole conception.

2. Military skill does not demand philosophic wisdom.

B. Philosophers are unfitted for important affairs.

1. This is shown by the examples of Socrates, Plato, and others.

2. [Refutation] Plato's philosopher-king has not been effective.

a. This is shown by the example of the Catos and others.

b. Even good kings leave the realm to bad sons.

c. [Digression] The wise are usually unfortunate in their children.

C. Philosophers are out of place in everyday occupations.

[12]   D. Civil society has been drawn and held together by folly and flattery.

E. The men who founded the arts were foolish.

[13] VI. Folly gives true prudence. (pp. 35-38)

A. Prudence in action requires rashness rather than consideration.

B. Even prudence in judgment is not what it is ordinarily thought to be.
  1. Things are not what they seem to be.
    a. Men but play parts in the world.
  2. A wise man from heaven who saw through the disguises would be imprudent.
  3. The really prudent man joins in acting the comedy, foolish as it may be.

[14] VII. Even wisdom is arrived at by way of folly. (pp. 38-43)
  A. The wise man pictured by the Stoics is a monster.
    1. He could not fit into a human world.
[15] B. Without folly, wisdom would lead to suicide.
    1. The life of man, as seen by the gods, is wretched.
    2. Old age would be intolerable without folly.
    3. Shame and infamy are not felt by fools.

[16] VIII. [Refutation] The argument that to be foolish is an unhappy state is untenable. (pp. 43-51)
  A. To be foolish is the natural state of man.
  B. It is not true that knowledge of the sciences increases man's happiness.
    1. The sciences were devised for man's harm.
    2. People of the golden age were happy without them.
    3. Among the sciences the more foolish are the more acceptable to mankind.
      a. Medicine is most acceptable, law is next, and theology, natural science, etc. are properly inacceptable.
  C. Among animals, those farthest from discipline are happiest.
    1. The bees are happy and admirable.
    2. The horse suffers from participation in human affairs.
    3. The cock in Lucian also proves this.
  D. Gryllus was happier than Odysseus, who forsook the guidance of nature.

[17]   E. Natural fools are the happiest of men.
- 1. They are free from fears and duties.
- 2. They enjoy the affection of everyone.
- 3. They enjoy the special favor of kings.
- 4. They can speak the truth without offense.
- 5. How happy they are may be seen by comparing them with scholars.

[18] IX. [Refutation] It is not true that madness is a form of wretchedness. (pp. 51-65)
- A. This argument ignores the distinction among kinds of madness.
  - 1. There is a benevolent madness.
    - a. Horace, Cicero, and others prove this.

[19]   B. Many kinds of madness are harmlessly pleasurable.
- 1. Such are the crazes for hunting, building, alchemy.
- 2. Gamblers are either harmlessly mad or else under the spell of the Furies.
- 3. People who hear and tell monstrous stories are harmlessly mad.

[20]   4. People who believe that charms and prayers to saints will help them are mad.
- a. Reprobates who expect the payment of a small sum to wipe out their offenses must be mad.
- b. People pray to be assisted in, rather than delivered from, their follies.
- c. To tell them that a good life is more effectual would make them unhappy.
- 5. People who arrange for their own funerals and those who glory in their ancestry are harmlessly mad.

[21]   C. All people are pleased by self-love.
- 1. Artists especially demonstrate this.
- 2. Cities and races enjoy self-love.

    D. Flattery also deludes men in a commendable way.

        1. Flattery is wrongly linked with deceit.

           a. The dog and squirrel flatter, yet are faithful.

        2. True flattery proceeds from kindness.

        3. True flattery has only good effects.

           a. It makes people feel better.

           b. It produces eloquence, medicine, and poetry.

[22]   E. The really sad thing is not to be deceived.

        1. The mind is more taken with appearances than realities.

           a. Solid matter in a sermon displeases, while fables please.

        2. Illusion is a cheap and easily available pleasure.

        3. Not to be deceived is to be lonely.

[23] X. Folly is greater than the other gods. (pp. 65-67)

    A. Her consolations are preferable to those of Bacchus.

    B. Other gods are fickle and partial in favor, while she is constant and impartial.

    C. Other gods require special worship and sacrifices.

    D. Though she has no temples of stone, all men are her living temples.

    E. She is worshipped more sincerely than are the Virgin and the saints.

        1. People worship only their images and do not exemplify their teachings and virtues.

    F. She is worshipped in all places.

[24] XI. All people are followers of Folly. (pp. 67-103)

    A. The gods use the spectacle of mankind as an entertainment.

    B. Merchants are special devotees of the goddess.

[25]   C. Even people accounted wise are her devotees.
       1. Grammarians would be wretched except for their folly.
         a. Their pains are mitigated by their sense of power over schoolboys.
         b. They are happy in their affectation of scholarship.
         c. The composing of poetry pleases them.
         d. Their preoccupation with fine distinctions pleasantly occupies their time.
       2. Poets are of Folly's faction.
       3. Rhetoricians belong to Folly's party.
         a. They reduce joking to an art.

[26]   4. Authors are kept happy by their follies.
         a. Authors with sound learning are unhappy.
         b. Popularity is a function of folly.
         c. Plagiarists are happy for a time.
         d. Popular authors are immersed in folly.
            (1) They are conceited.
            (2) They use cryptic titles and pseudonyms.
            (3) They trade compliments.
            (4) They maintain rivalries just to keep before the public.

[27]   5. Men of the learned professions succeed through folly.
         a. Lawyers make a false show of erudition.
         b. Logicians and sophists may be put with the lawyers.
         c. Scientists deal in follies.
            (1) They claim to know what cannot be known.
            (2) They do not know the truth.
               (a) Each disagrees with the others.

[28]   d. Theologians depend upon folly for their happiness.
            (1) They are happy in their self-love.

    (2) They multiply useless distinctions and definitions.

    (3) They play with abstruse questions.

    (4) They lay down absurd ethical rules.

    (5) They do not express realities as did the apostles.

    (6) They emend and criticize the church fathers.

    (7) They do not convert the heathen as did the apostles.

[29]   (8) Men of sound divinity are disgusted by them.

    (9) They believe they uphold the church.

    (10) They make their own pictures of hell and heaven.

    (11) They use a language of their own.

    (12) They glory in the title of "Our Masters."

[30] 6. The follies of monks make them happy.

    a. Although people dislike them, they are self-satisfied.

    b. They do not bother with learning.

    c. They can live by begging.

    d. They do everything by rule.

    e. Each order takes delight in its distinguishing marks.

    f. They deceive themselves as to the efficacy of these things.

      (1) Christ will judge by a different standard.

    g. Nobody dares treat them with contempt.

      (1) They have power through the confessional and through preaching.

[31]   h. Their preaching is absurd.

      (1) They use an invocation, like the poets.

(2) They use far-fetched exordia. [Digression concerning other preachers]
(3) They neglect the narration.
(4) They are pretentious in their argument.
(5) They use a silly story in the peroration.
(6) They follow ignorantly and blindly rhetorical rules of delivery.

   i. Women and merchants are pleased by their preaching.

[32] 7. Kings and courtiers worship folly.

   a. Folly makes a king's position tolerable.

      (1) A king conscious of his duties would be careworn and conscience-stricken.

   b. Courtiers give over all their days to foolish occupations and concerns.

[33] 8. Bishops, cardinals, and popes imitate kings and courtiers.

   a. A bishop who thought of the meaning of his garb and title would be condemned to irksome labor.

   b. A cardinal who took his duties seriously would be willing to give up his office.

   c. A pope who had a grain of wisdom would not be happy in his position.

   d. Popes, by lacking wisdom, lead a pleasant life.

      (1) They keep up the forms of religion only.

      (2) They maintain Peter's patrimony by the use of penalties.

      (3) They go to war as they please.

  9. Priests have a similar brand of folly.

   a. They also go to war—for tithes.

   b. They are satisfied with maintaining the forms of worship.

           c. They pass on the performance of religious duties to others.

[34] XII. Fortune favors fools. (pp. 103-104)

    A. This is shown by classic examples and proverbs.

    B. Wisdom is no aid in getting wealth.

    C. Fools are lucky in being more attractive to women than are wise men.

    D. Good fortune goes with money, which wise men shun.

[35] XIII. Great authorities exalt folly. (pp. 104-118)

    A. Proverbs commend even an imitation of it.

    B. Horace, Homer, and Cicero make favorable allusions to it.

    C. Sacred writers commend it.

        1. Solomon, Jeremiah, Ecclesiasticus, and Paul give various commendations of it.

[36]   2. Interpreters vainly try to wrench their words to another meaning.

            a. [Digression] Biblical interpreters make great mistakes.

                (1) Nicholas Lyra is a case in point.

                (2) Other interpreters commit absurdities.

[37]   D. Christ himself speaks of His foolishness.

    E. [Digression] Fools are acceptable to God.

    F. Christ favored the foolish of the world above the wise.

        1. His followers are called sheep.

        2. He is the Lamb of God.

        3. He became, in a manner, a fool in taking upon Him the nature of man.

        4. He recommends that His apostles speak without previous study.

    G. The forbidden Tree of Knowledge shows that wisdom is not for man.

    H. The Scriptures abundantly show that folly excuses transgressions.

1. Aaron, Saul, and David made foolishness an effectual excuse.
2. Christ asked pardon for His ignorant enemies.
3. Paul obtained mercy for what he did in ignorance.

[38] XIV. The Christian religion is akin to folly. (pp. 118-124)
    A. Children, women, the aged, and fools flock to church.
    B. The founders of the Church were enemies to learning.
    C. Zealous Christians are manifest fools.
       1. They give away their goods, forgive injuries, etc., in opposition to common sense.

[39]   D. The ultimate happiness sought by Christians is a kind of madness.
       1. Earthly preparations for this ultimate happiness partake of madness.
          a. For the soul to be uneasy in the body is madness.
          b. Other people see the spiritual aims and contemplations of Christians as madness.
          c. Holy men lose their physical perceptions, appetites, and affections.
          d. The pious take more account of the invisible than of the visible.
          e. Christians are like Plato's lovers.
             (1) They are absent from themselves.
       2. The heavenly consummation of this happiness accords with our definition of madness.
          a. The spirit first overmasters and swallows up the body.
          b. The spirit loses itself in the Supreme Mind.
       3. Moments of vision vouchsafed to the pious partake of madness.
          a. The pious soul is rapt from the body.
          b. The person becomes incoherent.

      c. Afterwards, he cannot remember what happened.

      d. He knows only that he was happy.

Peroration (p. 125)

[40]   I. Folly makes no summary because she cannot remember what she has said.

     II. Let votaries of Folly go on doing as they have done.

Notes

THE FOLLOWING NOTES SUPPLEMENT THE INFOR-
mation to be found in the "Index of Proper
Names." Sources are given for important
quotations. Erasmus's Latin often contains
phrases, though not so indicated, from Horace,
Cicero, Virgil, or Martial, and he frequently uses a single
unusual Greek word or pair of words from Lucian,
Aristophanes, or Homer. To annotate all of these echoes
would be of no special service. The interested student will
find most of them traced to their sources in the scholarly
edition of *Moriae Encomion* by I. J. Kan (The Hague,
1898). The proverbs Folly used are to be found, with commentary, in Erasmus's *Adagia*; those already clear in
meaning have been left unannotated here. All passages
from the Bible are annotated. Erasmus used the Vulgate,
but did not always quote accurately; in the text his Latin
has been closely translated, and in the Notes will be
found the corresponding passages as they appear in the
King James version.

PAGE

2 *great authors . . . Grunius Corocotta*] Erasmus combines, in his list,
mock-epics or other *jeux d'esprit* by poets and romancers with mock-
eulogies by rhetoricians. The poems he refers to are the pseudo-
Homeric *Batrachomyomachia* or "Battle of the Frogs and the Mice," the
Culex and *Moretum* which were attributed in his time to Virgil without
question, and Ovid's *Nux*, now considered non-Ovidian. Seneca has
traditionally been held author of *Apocolocyntosis*, or *Ludus de Morte Claudii*,
translated as "The Pumpkinification of Claudius," a satire upon the
apotheoses of emperors. For the other pieces see Index.

[143]

NOTES

4 *June 9th*] omitting the year given in the 1703 text, 1508, which is
plainly wrong, though introduced in Froben's edition of 1522. It should
probably be 1510, with 1511, the year of publication, as possible; 1509
is virtually impossible, unless "June" is in error. The composition of the
piece seems to belong to the late summer or autumn of 1509.

10 *imitate the rhetoricians*] The practice of using Greek words and phrases
in Latin compositions prevailed in academic oratory and writing
throughout the sixteenth century. In *The Praise of Folly* Erasmus uses
Greek more than eighty times, most frequently in the early pages.

16 *Sophocles . . . happiest*"] *Ajax*, line 554, translated by Trevelyan,
"For the life that is unconscious is most sweet."

18 *old gentleman in Plautus*] Demipho in *Mercator*, II, ii, 31-33, tells
Lysimachus that he has begun going to school and has learned three
letters; when Lysimachus asks, in surprise, what three letters, he replies,
"a-m-o." Erasmus does not name the letters, here inserted by the translator.

19 *people of Brabant*] Kan gives this Dutch proverb concerning Brabanters
and Hollanders:

> Hoe ouder, hoe zotter Brabander;
> Hoe ouder, hoe botter Hollander.

I.e., "The older the foolisher, the Brabanter; the older the stupider, the
Hollander."

20 *daughter of Memnon . . . Tithonus*] Erasmus seems to err, since it is
usually accounted that Aurora, mother of Memnon and consort of
Tithonus, restored his youth.

23 *Plato shows . . . rational creatures*] An example of Folly's wresting of
evidence, if *Republic*, V, 451, is referred to, as seems most likely. The
question there is whether women shall undertake the duties of guardians
of the state along with men. A figure is drawn from animals, but men are
included in the figure; in Davis's translation: "Are we to reckon it
proper for the females among our guardian dogs to watch and hunt,
and do everything in common with the males; or rather to manage
domestic affairs within doors, as being disabled from other exercises on
account of bearing and nursing the whelps, while the males are to labor
and take the entire charge of the flock? . . . Is it possible . . . to
employ an animal for the same purpose [with another] without giving
it the same nurture and education?"

23 *bull to the masseuse*] The Latin is *ad ceroma*, that is, to the anointing-
place of athletes.

NOTES

26 *ambiguous syllogisms*] *Crocodiletes*, a kind of syllogism, according to the note of Listrius in the 1515 edition, named from the story of a crocodile which offered terms to the mother of a boy it had seized: "If you will tell me the truth," it said, "I will return your boy to you." She answered, "You will not return him. Now, since I have told the truth, return him." The crocodile answered, "No, if I were to return him, you would not have spoken the truth."

26 *none is born . . . of them*] Though not so indicated, Erasmus is virtually quoting Horace, *Satires*, I, iii, 68-69.

30 *poetic sentiment of Archilochus*] In Plutarch's *Instituta Laconica*, 34, translated by Babbitt, Loeb Classical Library: "Archilochus the poet, when he arrived in Sparta, they ordered to depart that very instant because they learned that he had written in his verses that it is better to throw away one's arms than be killed."

31 *struck dumb . . . a wolf*] The Latin expression *lupus in fabula* or *lupus in sermone* corresponds to our "Talk of the devil—" and indicates that, since the person being talked about has appeared, the speaker breaks off in embarrassment.

32 *Quintilian interprets*] *Institutes*, XI, i, 43-44; but Quintilian rather cites than commends Cicero here.

32 *saying of Plato's*] *Republic*, V, 473.

33 *wolf in the story*] See note to similar expression, above, p. 31.

34 *puerile story . . . horses' tails*] (1) Livy tells (I, ii) that the Roman fathers overcame a seditious uprising by sending the orator Menenius Agrippa to speak to the people; he told the fable of how the members grumbled and mutinied against the belly, but when they found, with the sustenance provided by the belly cut off, that they grew weak, they were reconciled to their former position and duties. (2) The fable of the fox and hedgehog, used by Themistocles as an argument against changing governments, appears in Aristotle, *Rhetoric*, II, 20: the fox, mired in a bog and assailed by ticks, refused to allow the hedgehog to remove them, on the ground that these already had their fill of blood, whereas if they were removed the new ticks that would follow would be empty and ravenous. (3) Sertorius, in Plutarch's *Lives*, was a noble Roman general who pretended that his white hind had been given him by Diana and that it gave him valuable information about the plans of the enemy. (4) In Plutarch's *De Puerorum Educatione* is told the experiment of Lycurgus ("the Spartan") with "identical twins": he took two puppies of the same litter and had them reared separately and differently, so that one became fierce and intractable, the other an obedient and skil-

NOTES

ful hunter. (5) The last object-lesson comes also from Plutarch's account of Sertorius: to prove that good strategy could do more than mere strength, he set two men to pull out, respectively, the tails of two horses; one tried to pull the tail out all at once, and failed; the other, pulling a hair at a time, succeeded.

36 *Homer seems . . . is done"*] *Iliad*, XVII, 32, translated by Lang, Leaf, and Myers: "By the event is even a fool made wise."

36 *fat Minerva*] To do something *crassa Minerva* or *pingue Minerva* (with a stupid, or fat, Minerva) means, in Horace and elsewhere, to do it awkwardly or without niceties.

37 *king . . . hostler*] The word translated "hostler" is *Dama*, a type-name used by Horace (*Satires*, I, vi; II, v) and Persius (Satire V) for a low-born or mean fellow; apparently it was a name often given to slaves.

41 *Aristophanes . . . toolless"*] *Plutus*, 266-67.

42 *borrowed teeth . . . pig*] The translation here departs from the 1703 text and follows many earlier editions in reading *a sue* where 1703 has *a se*; to follow 1703 would give: "another enjoys the use of teeth he has got somewhere as a loan."

45 *"The doctor . . . together"*] This line from the *Iliad*, XI, 514, Erasmus may have seen quoted in Plato's *Symposium*, 214B.

49 *Alcibiades in Plato*] *Symposium*, 217E.

49 *Euripides witnesseth . . . things"*] *Bacchae*, 369.

49 *Euripides mentions*] Kan suggests line 394 of the pseudo-Euripidean *Rhesus*, where "double men" are mentioned.

51 *Socrates teaches . . . two Venuses*] Pausanius, rather than Socrates, is represented as making this distinction, *Symposium*, 180.

51 *Horace . . . upon me"*] *Odes*, III, iv, 5-6.

52 *Cicero . . . Atticus*] Folly twists the evidence, unless Erasmus himself was mistaken. The passage referred to must be from the letters to Atticus, III, xiii, 2: *Nam, quod scribis te audire me etiam mentis errore ex dolore adfici, mihi vero mens integra est. Atque utinam tam in periculo fuisset!* In the Loeb translation by Winstedt: "You say that you have heard that my mind is becoming unhinged with grief: my mind is sound enough. Would that it had been as sound in the hour of danger, . . ." Only if the last expression is made to refer, as it can hardly do, to the earlier part of the preceding sentence, so that it would mean, "Would that it had been unhinged in the hour of danger," can Folly's interpretation be justified.

52 *that Greek in Horace*] Erasmus follows closely Horace's account, *Epistles* II. ii, 128-40.

NOTES

57 *seven verses . . . St. Bernard*] The story was that a devil appeared to
St. Bernard and told him that there were seven verses in the *Psalms*, the
daily repetition of which would insure a person's salvation. St. Bernard
replied that he would repeat all of the *Psalms* daily and thus be sure of
saying the seven verses. The devil was so disconcerted by this suggestion
that he revealed the effective verses.

58 *"For if I . . . folly"*] Erasmus adapts three lines of Virgil, *Aeneid*, VI,
625-27; but where Virgil speaks of crimes and punishments (in connection with Aeneas's visit to the underworld), Erasmus substitutes fools
and folly.

59 *King Arthur*] The Latin is *Arcturum*, and perhaps the translation should
be "the star Arcturus." For translating as "King Arthur" we have this:
Erasmus was writing in England, and he has said that some people trace
their ancestry to Aeneas or to Brutus. A Brutus, supposed to have been
a grandson of Aeneas, was the legendary founder of Britain; but at the
time Erasmus wrote there was a tendency to exalt King Arthur, particularly because the Tudor kings, of Welsh extraction, were willing to
believe they were in Arthur's descent. King Henry VII named his first
son Arthur. Also, *Arcturus* is a possible variant of *Arturus*. For translating
as "the star Arcturus" we have Kan's suggestion that Erasmus had in
mind the phrase from Cicero, *De Natura Deorum*, II, xlii, 110, *Stella
micans radiis, Arcturus nomine claro*.

 Wilson translates, "the Star by the Tail of Ursa Major"; Kennett,
"king Arthur."

64 *a man of my name*] Thomas More, as the puns on More and Moria in the
Preface indicate.

65 *And of course . . . hangmen*] Kan points out that many editors, but
without good authority, insert a *non* before the verb of this sentence;
Wilson so translates: "to say nothing of those mischievous gods, Plutoes,
Ates," etc.

70 *curses . . . Greek epigram*] *Greek Anthology*, IX, 173, by Palladas of
Alexandria (tr. by Paton, Loeb Classical Library): "The beginning of
grammar [i.e., of the *Iliad*] is a curse in five lines. The first has the word
'wrath,' the second 'pernicious,' and after that 'many woes' of the
Greeks; the third 'leads down souls to Hades'; to the fourth belong
'spoil' and 'dogs'; to the fifth 'birds' of ill-omen and the 'anger of Zeus.'
How, then, can a grammarian avoid having many sorrows after five
curses and five cases (falls)?"

71 *ass in Aesop*] Perhaps in the fable of the ass in the lion's skin; though
the fable of the ass attempting to be a lap-dog would answer as well.

[147]

NOTES

71 *bubsequa . . . manticulator*] The three words, of rare or obscure occurrence, mean, respectively, "herdsman," "blusterer" or "tergiversator," and "pickpocket."

73 *free souls . . . proverb*] The proverb is phrased by Horace, *Epistola ad Pisones* ("Art of Poetry"), 9-10: *Pictoribus atque poetis / Quidlibet audendi semper fuit aequa potestas.* Lucian alludes to the saying in his *Defence of the Portraits,* 18.

79-80 *"Faith is . . . not seen"*] *Hebrews,* xi, 1, as here.

80 *"God is . . . in truth"*] *John* iv, 24, as here.

81 "strifes of words"] 2 *Timothy* ii, 14: "charging them before the Lord that they strive not about words to no profit"; *ibid.,* 23: "But foolish and unlearned questions avoid, knowing that they do gender strifes." For genealogies, mentioned a little earlier, see 1 *Timothy,* i, 4.

84 *matula putes . . . ollam fervere*] The meaning of the phrases is of no special pertinence: the first might be translated as "pot, you stink," the second as "the pot stinks"; *ollae fervere* is of no recognizable construction, but may possibly have been intended to represent the meaning of our phrase, "to boil the kettle"; *ollam fervere* is simply "the kettle boils."

85 *"ineffable Four Letters"*] In Hebrew tradition, four consonants which represented the name of God, not to be pronounced; Jehovah.

89 *Horace,* "What . . . about?"] *Satires,* II, vii, 21: *quorsum haec tam putida tendant?*

91 *imitating . . . Sagana*] The allusion is to Horace, *Satires,* I, viii, in which Priapus tells of witnessing the nocturnal rites and sorceries of Canidia and Sagana, women represented as hag-like witches. At the height of the ceremonies Priapus broke wind.

91 *august titles . . . Invincible Doctors*] Erasmus is satirizing the custom of giving epithets to well-known theologians; Thomas Aquinas was "the angelic doctor," Duns Scotus was "the subtle doctor," William of Occam was "the invincible doctor," St. Francis was "the seraphic father."

92 *their chimera . . . Humano capite, etc.*] The reference is to the opening of Horace's *Epistola ad Pisones* (*Epistles,* II, iii), usually called his "Art of Poetry." He is warning against incongruity in poetry and draws an analogy from painting (tr. by Lonsdale and Lee): "If a painter were to try to unite a man's head on a horse's neck, or to put parti-colored feathers on limbs collected from every kind of animal, so that, for instance, a woman fair to the waist were to end foul in the tail of an ugly fish; if admitted to view, my friends, could you restrain your laughter?" The Latin begins: *Humano capite cervicem pictor equinam.*

NOTES

96 *"suitors of Penelope . . . Echo*] Erasmus refers to Horace, *Epistles*, I, ii, 28*ff*. The particular verse he begins to quote is *sponsi Penelopae, nebulones Alcinoique,* and the whole passage reads (tr. by Lonsdale and Lee): "Penelope's suitors, and the young courtiers of Alcinous, who employed themselves more than was proper in attending to their bodily pleasures; who thought it seemly to slumber till noon, and to charm their care to sink to rest at the music of the lyre." The suitors are similarly described in the *Odyssey*, II, 74*ff*. The statement that Echo can give the other half of the verse is obscure; Erasmus may be suggesting that the word *nebulones* gives the echo ὄνος, Greek for "ass," or that the ending of *Alcinoique* sounds like "Echo." In his colloquy entitled "Echo" he twice uses oblique forms of ὄνος as an echo, first for *eruditionis* and then for *Cicerone*.

97 *what . . . "bishop" means*] The word "bishop" is from the Greek, ἐπίσκοπος, overseer, inspector, or guardian.

100 *weapons and sweet benedictions*] 2 *Corinthians* vi, 4, 6-7: "But in all things approving ourselves as the ministers of God . . . by pureness, by knowledge, by long-suffering, by kindness, by the Holy Ghost, by love unfeigned, by the word of truth, by the power of God, by the armor of righteousness on the right hand and on the left." For weapons, cf. *Romans* xiii, 12: "let us therefore cast off the works of darkness, and let us put on the armor of light"; *2 Corinthians* x, 4: "For the weapons of our warfare are not carnal, but mighty through God to the pulling down of strongholds"; *Ephesians* vi, 11-17, describing "the whole armor of God," and naming the several weapons. For blessings, cf. also *Romans* xii, 14: "Bless them which persecute you: bless and curse not."

F. M. Nichols, in *The Epistles of Erasmus* (1904), II, 7, translates this part of the sentence, "There remain only arms, and those 'fair speeches' of which Paul makes mention," and cites (following Kan) *Romans* xvi, 18. But so to translate is to lose the irony of the passage; and the quotations listed above justify an ironical reading.

100 *pictured damnations*] A note by Listrius, in the Basle, 1515, edition, explains that pictures were sometimes published of those whom the Pope excommunicated, showing them surrounded by flame and devils.

100 *Peter's . . . followed thee"*] *Matthew* xix, 27.

103 *"The owl flies"*] A proverbial token of victory in Athens; the owl was Athena's bird.

103 *"He . . . fourth month"*] A portent of a difficult, laborious life, because Hercules was supposed to have been born in that month.

NOTES

105 *fat, sleek hog . . . season"*] Erasmus is referring to Horace's **own** words concerning himself. The pertinent passages, including the following quotations, are as follows (translated by Lonsdale and Lee): *Epistles* I, iv, 15-16: "Myself you will find plump and sleek, in high condition, when you wish to laugh at a hog from the sty of Epicurus"; *Odes*, IV, xii, 27-28: "mix with your meditations a brief folly; 'tis sweet **at** fitting time to lose our wisdom." Erasmus errs in attributing the second quotation to "elsewhere."

105 *"had rather be giddy . . . fret"*] Horace, *Epistles*, II, ii, 126-28 (translated by Lonsdale and Lee): "But yet, better be thought a silly and dull poet, provided my own faults please me, or at least escape me, than to be ever so sensible, and to chafe in one's spirit."

105 *Cicero . . . fools"*] *Epistolae ad Familiares*, IX, xxii, 4.

106 *"The number . . . infinite"*] *Ecclesiastes* i, 15: "that which is wanting cannot be numbered." The Latin of the Vulgate is as Erasmus quotes it: *stultorum infinitus est numerus.*

106 *"Every man . . . wisdom"*] *Jeremiah* x, 14: "Every man is brutish in his knowledge."

106 *"Let not . . . wisdom"*] *Jeremiah* ix, 23: "Let not the wise man glory in his wisdom."

106 *"Vanity . . . vanity"*] *Ecclesiastes* i, 2: "Vanity of vanities, saith the Preacher, vanity of vanities; all is vanity." Also xii, 8.

107 *"the fool is . . . sun"*] *Ecclesiasticus* xxvii, 12: "The discourse of a godly man is always with wisdom, but a fool's changeth as the moon." The Latin of the Vulgate contains a reference to the sun: *Homo sanctus in sapientia manet sicut sol,* etc.

107 *"A fool . . . folly"*] *Proverbs* xv, 21: "Folly is joy to him that is destitute of wisdom."

107 *"He that . . . grief"*] *Ecclesiastes* i, 18: "For in much wisdom is much grief; and he that increaseth knowledge increaseth sorrow."

107 *"The heart . . . follows mirth"*] *Ecclesiastes* vii, 4: "The heart of the wise is in the house of mourning; but the heart of fools is in the house of mirth."

107 *"I gave . . . folly"*] *Ecclesiastes* i, 17, as here.

108 *"Buckets . . . Aristotle]* Erasmus means, obviously, that cheap, common vessels are left carelessly about; but as Aristotle used the proverb in his *Rhetoric* (I, 6) the meaning was not this. The following is Lane Cooper's translation and (in brackets) his comment: "And hence, too, the proverb about 'breaking the pitcher at the door' [after the trouble and toil of filling and fetching it]."

NOTES

108 *"Better is . . . wisdom"*] *Ecclesiasticus* xx, 33: "Better is he that hideth his folly than a man that hideth his wisdom."

108 *"A fool . . . fools"*] *Ecclesiastes* x, 3: "Yea also, when he that is a fool walketh by the way, his wisdom faileth him, and he saith to every one that he is a fool."

108 *"I am . . . men"*] *Proverbs* xxx, 2: "Surely I am more brutish than any man, and have not the understanding of a man."

108-9 *"I speak . . . more"*] Because of the extended discussion, the context may be given; *2 Corinthians* xi, 21-23: "I speak as concerning reproach, as though we had been weak. Howbeit whereinsoever any is bold, (I speak foolishly) I am bold also. Are they [i.e., "false apostles, deceitful workers, transforming themselves into apostles of Christ"] Hebrews? so am I. Are they Israelites? so am I. Are they the seed of Abraham? so am I. Are they ministers of Christ? (I speak as a fool) I am more; in labors more abundant, in stripes above measure, in prisons more frequent, in deaths oft."

109 *a certain renowned divine*] As the proverb presently quoted indicates, Erasmus refers to Nicholas de Lyra; see Index.

110 *"to the Unknown God"*] *Acts* xvii, 23: "For as I passed by, and beheld your devotions, I found an altar with this inscription, TO THE UNKNOWN GOD. Whom therefore ye ignorantly worship, him declare I unto you."

111 *"But now, he . . . one"*] With context, *Luke* xxii, 35-36: "And he said unto them, When I sent you without purse, and scrip, and shoes, lacked ye anything? And they said, Nothing. Then said he unto them, But now he that hath a purse, let him take it, and likewise his scrip: and he that hath no sword, let him sell his garment and buy one." In the exegesis put in the mouth of Folly, Erasmus seems to imply that *tollat* (translated in the text as "take") means "remove" or "dispense with." The word allows such an interpretation, since its meaning embraces both "take up" or "carry" and "take away" or "remove."

113 *"the skins . . . shaken"*] *Habakkuk* iii, 7: "I saw the tents of Cushan in affliction: and the curtains of the land of Midian did tremble."

113 *"A man . . . reject"*] *Titus* iii, 10, as here. The story Erasmus tells about the interpretation of *devita* is a true one, told to him, according to his note on this verse in his New Testament, by John Colet, who had heard the interpretation made.

113 *the word . . . devita*] This phrase inserted by the translator.

113 *"Thou shalt . . . to live"*] *Exodus* xxii, 18, as here.

114 *using maleficus as above*] Inserted by the translator.

[151]

NOTES

114 *"Suffer fools gladly"*] 2 Corinthians xi, 19: "For ye suffer fools gladly, seeing ye yourselves are wise."

114 *"Receive me as a fool"*] 2 Corinthians xi, 16: "I say again, let no man think me a fool; if otherwise, yet as a fool receive me, that I may boast myself a little."

114 *"I do not . . . foolishness"*] 2 Corinthians xi, 17: "That which I speak, I speak it not after the Lord, but as it were foolishly, in this confidence of boasting."

114 *"We are fools for Christ's sake"*] 1 Corinthians iv, 10, as here.

114 *"Let him . . . wise"*] 1 Corinthians iii, 18: "If any man among you seemeth to be wise in this world, let him become a fool, that he may be wise."

114 *two disciples . . . "fools"*] Luke xxiv, 25: "Then he said unto them, O fools, and slow of heart to believe all that the prophets have spoken."

114 *"The foolishness . . . men"*] 1 Corinthians i, 25, as here.

114 *"The preaching . . . foolishness"*] 1 Corinthians i, 18, as here.

115 *"Thou knowest my foolishness"*] Psalms lxix, 5, as here; usually taken, however, as the psalmist's personal expression.

115 *"God has . . . world"*] 1 Corinthians i, 27: "But God hath chosen the foolish things of the world to confound the wise."

115 *"It has . . . foolishness"*] 1 Corinthians i, 21: "For after that in the wisdom of God the world by wisdom knew not God, it pleased God by the foolishness of preaching to save them that believe."

115 *"I will destroy . . . prudent"*] Isaiah xxix, 14: "for the wisdom of their wise men shall perish, and the understanding of their prudent men shall be hid."

115 *gave thanks . . . babes*] Matthew xi, 25: "I thank thee, O Father, Lord of heaven and earth, because thou hast hid these things from the wise and prudent, and hast revealed them unto babes."

115 *"Woe unto . . . Pharisees"*] Luke xi, 44, as here; cf. xii, 42, 43, and Matthew xxiii, 27.

116 *"Behold the Lamb of God"*] John i, 29 and 36, as here.

116 *"the wisdom of the Father"*] 1 Corinthians i, 24: "But unto them which are called, both Jews and Greeks, Christ the power of God, and the wisdom of God." See also i, 18.

116 *made "to be sin"*] 2 Corinthians v, 21: "For he hath made him to be sin for us, who knew no sin; that we might be made the righteousness of God in him."

116 *"the foolishness of the cross"*] Not a quotation; Kan suggests it is adapted from "the foolishness of preaching," 1 Corinthians i, 21; more

NOTES

likely, however, from *Galatians* v, 11; "Then is the offense of the cross ceased," or *1 Corinthians* i, 18: "For the preaching of the cross is to them that perish foolishness," or i, 23: "But we preach Christ crucified . . . unto the Greeks foolishness."

117 *mountain . . . Lucifer*] *Isaiah* xiv, 12, 13: "How art thou fallen from heaven, O Lucifer . . . For thou hast said in thine heart . . . I will sit also upon the mount of the congregation."

117 *"I beseech . . . charge"*] *Numbers* xii, 11: "And Aaron said unto Moses, Alas, my lord, I beseech thee, lay not the sin upon us, wherein we have done foolishly, and wherein we have sinned."

117 *"For it . . . foolishly"*] *1 Samuel* xxvi, 21: "Behold, I have played the fool, and have erred exceedingly."

117 *"But I pray . . . foolishly"*] *1 Chronicles* xxi, 8: "But now, I beseech thee, do away the iniquity of thy servant; for I have done very foolishly."

117 *"Father, forgive . . . do"*] *Luke* xxiii, 34, as here.

117 *"But therefore . . . unbelief"*] *1 Timothy* i, 13: "but I obtained mercy, because I did it ignorantly in unbelief."

118 *"Remember not . . . ignorances"*] *Psalms* xxv, 7: "Remember not the sins of my youth, nor my transgressions."

119 *Plato defined . . . death"*] *Phaedo*, 80-81.

123 *Plato . . . state of all"*] *Phaedrus*, 244.

124 *"Eye hath not . . . Him"*] *1 Corinthians* ii, 9, as here.

124 *that "good part . . . away"*] The Latin is *haec est Moriae pars, quae non aufertur*, etc. That there is a serious pun intended between *Moriae* and *Mariae*, identifying "the portion of Folly" with that "good part" chosen by Mary, sister of Martha, in *Luke* x, 42, is indicated by *quae non aufertur*, which resembles the wording of the Vulgate. In English the verse reads: "But one thing is needful: and Mary hath chosen that good part, which shall not be taken away from her." Most texts consulted, including those of best authority, read *Moriae pars. Mariae* is the reading, however, of the edition printed by Jacob Mark, Leyden, 1627, and the Oxford edition of 1663 (wrongly dated, 1633). This last may account for the fact that Wilson translates the phrase as "that Mary's better part"; Kennett, as "that better part which Mary chose."

Index of Proper Names

WITH THE NAMES APPEARS A MINIMUM OF explanation pertinent to Erasmus's use of them; (note) after a page-reference indicates that additional comment will be found in the Notes, introduced by that page-number. References to the Deity and to Folly herself, are omitted, as are the names of gods when used in oaths, books of the Bible, and a few capitalized adjectives.

Aaron, 117 (note)

Academics, philosophic followers of Plato or of the later Platonic Academies, 63

Acarnania, part of Epirus in Greece, the modern Carnia, classically famous for its pigs, 19

Achilles, 18, 47

Adam, 80

Ad Herennium, a Latin instruction-book in rhetoric, for long attributed to Cicero; by Erasmus's time his authorship was questioned, 73

Adonis, gardens of, for long a proverbial and poetic expression for beautiful pleasure-gardens, 12

Aeneas, 51, 59 (note)

Aesop, 71 (note)

Africa, 71

Ajax, 47

Albertists, scholastic followers of Albertus Magnus, a Bavarian schoolman of the thirteenth century, 79, 82

Alcaeus, Greek lyric poet of the seventh century B.C., 75

Alcibiades, young nobleman of Athens, friend to Socrates and one of the interlocutors in Plato's *Symposium*, where he drew the analogy from the images of Silenus, 36, 49

Aldus, Aldo Manuzio, or Aldus Manutius (1450-1515), Venetian scholar and printer, founder of the Aldine Press; Erasmus had been living and working with him just before writing this book; the reference to him is jocular, 72

Amphion, legendary Greek musician, supposed to have brought together, by playing his lyre, stones for the original walls of Thebes; his musical power is sometimes rationalized, as here, to mean eloquence, 34

Anagyris foetida, the bean trefoil, proverbial for its unsavoriness, 77

Anchises, father of Aeneas in Virgil; the question about his mother is imitated from Juvenal's (Satier VII, 234) about the nurse of Anchises, and from Suetonius'

(*Tiberius*, lxx, 3) about the mother of Hecuba, 71

Anoia, or Madness, attendant of Folly, 13, 15

Anti-Joves, Latin *Vejoves; Vejovis* was a god having attributes the reverse of Jove's, 65

Anthonies, probably St. Anthony of Padua (1195-1231) is referred to, since he was famed for his eloquent preaching, 93

Antony, Marcus Antonius (B.C. 83-30), Roman general, 115

Apelles, famed Greek painter, fourth century B.C., 64

Aphrodite, cf. also Venus, 21

Apollo, cf. also Phoebus, 31, 65

Apuleius (Lucius), Roman satirist and philosopher (born ?125), author of *The Golden Ass*, 2

Archilochus, Greek poet, said to have been inventor of iambic satirical verse, 30 (note)

Argos, city of Peloponnesus, having Juno as tutelar goddess, 67

Argus, sentinel with a hundred eyes, appointed by Juno to watch Io when Jupiter was in love with her, 27, 68

Aristophanes, Greek writer of comedies (B.C. ?448-?380), among them Plutus, 12, 41

Aristotle, 34, 81, 108 (note), 116

Arthur, *King*, 59 (note)

Ate, goddess of revenge and discord, 21, 65

Athenian, 30

Athens, 32, 67

Atlas, 83

Atticus (T. Pomponius), friend of Cicero, 52

Augustine (St.), a father of the church (354-450), 84

Augustinians, members of orders following rule of Augustine, 87

Aurora, goddess of dawn, 19

Baal, 89

Babylon, 71

Babylonian, 89

Bacchus, 13, 20, 65

Barbara (St.), virgin and martyr of obscure tradition, 56, 63

Bartholomew (St.), one of the Apostles, supposed to have met his martyrdom by being flayed, 113

Basil (St.), a father of the church (?329-379), 82

Basilides, heretic of the second century, who constructed a system of 365 heavens; Erasmus's Latin, *Abraxasiorum coelos*, refers to the Abraxas, a numerical symbol or talisman of Basilides, 88

Benedictines, members of the congregation following the rule of St. Benedict of Nursia, instituted about 525, 87

Bernard (St.), cf. next entry, 57 (note), 117

Bernardines, members of the branch of the Cistercian order founded (1115) by St. Bernard of Clairvaux, 87

Brabant, formerly a duchy of Netherlands, later divided between Holland and Belgium, 19

Brabanters, 19 (note)

Bridgetines, members of an order founded by St. Bridget or Bride (453-523), patroness of Ireland; Kan points out that the form used by Erasmus, *Brigidenses*, indicates the Irish saint rather than St. Brigit or Birgitta of Sweden; otherwise, the translation should read Brigittines, 87

Brutus (legendary founder of Britain), 59 (note)

Brutus (Marcus Junius), Roman politician (B.C. 85-42), one of

INDEX OF PROPER NAMES

the assassins of Caesar; committed suicide, 32, 41, 115

Busiris, cruel Egyptian tyrant of the early Greek period; his name became a synonym for tyranny, 2, 9

Callimachus, Greek poet in Egypt (B.C. ?320-?240), librarian of Ptolemy II, 75

Camarina, *Lake*, a stinking lake in Sicily; people of the city near by drained the lake in spite of being forbidden to do so by Apollo; across the lake-bed enemies entered and sacked the city; hence the proverb, *Camarinam ne moveas*, meant "Be not the cause of thy own ruin," 77

Canidia, 91 (note)

Carthusians, members of an austere order founded in the Chartreuse, near Grenoble, France; Erasmus's respect for this order was shared by Thomas More who, as a young man, lived four years in the Charterhouse (Carthusian monastery) of London; Erasmus glances obliquely at the Carthusian practice of silence, 102

Cassius (Gaius), Roman leader, one of Caesar's assassins; committed suicide, B.C. 42, 32, 41, 115

Cato (Marcus Porcius), "the elder" (B.C. 234-149), also called "the censor"; the story was often told of his walking out of a theater in the midst of a performance, as a rebuke, 33

Cato (Marcus Porcius, of Utica), "the younger" (B.C. 95-46), philosopher, patriot and soldier; his suicide is graphically recounted by Plutarch, 41

Catos, the, see previous entries, 32

Chaldeans, classically considered inventors of astronomy and astrology, 44

Chaos, original disordered matter of the universe, personified as parent of the earliest gods, 11

Chiron, the centaur, teacher of Achilles and others; accidentally wounded by Hercules' arrow, he suffered but could not die, since he was immortal; wishing release from pain, he transferred his immortality to Prometheus; in Lucian's *Dialogues of the Dead* Chiron tells Menippus why he preferred not to be immortal, 41

Christopher (St.), patron saint of travellers, pictured bearing Christ (in the form of a child) on his shoulders; since he was drawn with but one eye showing and carrying a huge staff, Erasmus calls him Polyphemus, 56, 63

Chrysippean, cf. next entry, 81

Chrysippus, Stoic philosopher and logician, student of Zeno's, supposed to have written 705 works, 114

Chrysostom (St.), Greek father of the Church (?347-407), 82

Cicero (Marcus Tullius), 31, 32, 33, 52 (note), 75, 91, 93, 105 (note), 106

Cilician from Cilicia, a country in Asia Minor; cloth of Cilician goat's hair was coarse and rough, 86

Circe, sorceress in the *Odyssey*, X; changed men into beasts by her enchantments, 19

Claudius, Emperor, Tiberius Claudius Drusus Nero Germanicus (B.C. 10-A.D. 54), 2

Coletes, members of an order founded by St. Coleta (1380-1447), a lady of Picardy, 87

Comus, or Intemperance, attendant of Folly, 13

Cordeliers, members of the Franciscan order, so called from their girdles of knotted cord, 87

Croesus, Lydian king famed for his wealth, 53

Crutched, or Crossed (friars), members of an English order, so called because of crosses on their staves and garments, 87

Cupid, 21, 27, 51

Cyprus, 67

David, 117 (note)

Decii, the, an early Decius gave his life for Rome in the Latin War; his son did as much in the Estruscan War; and a grandson, in the war against Pyrrhus, 34

Delos, an island in the Aegean Sea, birthplace of Apollo and Diana, anciently thought to be a floating island, 12

Democritus, of Abdera (B.C. ?460-362), Greek atomistic philosopher, known as "the laughing philosopher," 2, 35, 67, 70

Demosthenes, Athenian orator (B.C. ?384-322), supposed to have fled from the battlefield of Chaeronea, 30, 32, 91, 93

Diana, 21, 66

Didymus, grammarian of the time of Augustus, supposed to have written 3000 or 4000 books, 114

Diogenes, the Cynic, philosopher of Athens; according to one of several stories (Diogenes Laertius VI, 76-77), he died voluntarily by holding his breath, 41

Dionysius, the name of two famous tyrants of Sicily; Plato gave advice concerning government to Dionysius the younger, and almost lost his life as a result, 71, 115

Dodona, city on the border of Thessaly, famous for its fountain and grove in which was a temple of Jupiter; the oracle answered by a wind through the trees, and brass vessels or gongs were hung on the trees to increase the sound, 76

Donatus (Aelius), Roman grammarian (fl. 305), whose work was a standard textbook throughout the Middle Ages, 71

Drunkenness, a nymph, nurse and attendant of Folly, 13

Echo, 96 (note)

Egypt, 89

Elysian Fields, 50

Endymion, young shepherd beloved of Diana, 21

England, 1

English, 61

Epicurus, Greek philosopher (B.C. ?342-270), founder of Epicurean school of thought, 105 (note)

Epidaurian serpent, Erasmus borrows both the eagle and the serpent from Horace, *Satires*, I, iii, 27; Epidauris was a city in Peloponnesus; the serpents were sacred to Aesculapius, 27

Erasmus (St.), the most prominent of the several saints of this name is Erasmus of Formia (called in Italy St. Elmo), a bishop in the region of Antioch, martyred in 303; the reference is of course equivocal, 56

Erasmus (Desiderius), 103, 109

Eucharist, the, sacrament central to the Mass, 78, 80, 122

Euclid, Greek philosopher, founder of geometry (fl. B.C. 400), 60

INDEX OF PROPER NAMES

Euripides, Greek writer of tragedies (B.C. 480-406), 49 (notes)

Fates, 41

Favorinus, Roman philosopher or Sophist living in Gaul, second century A.D., wrote eulogies of Thersites and the quartan fever, 2

Febris, goddess of fever, or averter of fever, 65

Festus, Roman provincial governor, who said after Paul's defence (*Acts* xxvi): "Paul, thou art beside thyself; much learning doth make thee mad," 119

Flora, Roman goddess of flowers, whose festival, was a time of licentiousness, 21

Fortunate Isles, in Greek and later legend, islands far in the western ocean, home of favored mortals on whom the gods had bestowed immortality, 12, 17, 30

Fortune, goddess of, 103

Frenchmen, 61

Furies, the, three in number, came from Hades to pursue and drive to madness people guilty of outrageous crimes, 51, 55, 100

George (St.), of Cappadocia, patron saint of England, of whom little is known; supposed to have lived in third and early fourth centuries, 56

Germans, 61 63, 101

Gesta Romanorum, "Deeds of the Romans," a Latin collection of tales and anecdotes compiled about 1300; an English translation was published by Wynkyn de Worde about the time *The Praise of Folly* was written, 91

Giants, sons of Titan and Tellus, waged an unsuccessful war against the Olympian gods, 47

Glaucon, made a case for injustice in the second book of Plato's *Republic*, 2

Gorgon, the head of Medusa, worn by Pallas on her shield, said to turn the beholder into stone, 21

Gracchi, the, Tiberius Gracchus (B.C. ?153-121) and his brother, Gaius Gracchus (B.C. ?162-133), liberal political leaders in Rome, killed as rousers of sedition, 32

Greeklings, translating *Graeculi*, Folly's contemptuous name for Biblical interpreters who know Greek; she puns with *graculi*, grackles, 109

Greeks, 10, 24, 27, 42, 44, 61, 65, 72

Grunnius Corocotta (Porcellus), fictional name of a pig, whose last will and testament was written in verse by an unknown author and, according to St. Jerome (ed. J.-P. Migne, *Patrologia Latina*, IV, 491), sung or recited by schoolboys, 2

Gryllus, subject of a dialogue by Plutarch, the interlocutors being Circe, Ulysses, and the talking pig, Gryllus, who formerly had been a man, 2, 47

Harpocrates, god of silence, 22

Hebrews, cf. also Jews, 85 (note), 90, 113

Hedone, or Pleasure, attendant of Folly, 13

Helicon, one of the peaks of Parnassus, home of Apollo and the Muses, 38, 105

Hercules, 8, 56

Hermogenes, Marcus Hermogenes Tigellius, a remarkable Roman singer, friend of Julius and Augustus Caesar, often mentioned by Horace; see especially *Satires*, I, ix, 25, 60

INDEX OF PROPER NAMES

Hesiod, one of the earliest Greek poets, fl. eighth century B.C., 11

Hippolytus, son of Theseus, killed when fleeing from his father, restored to life by Aesculapius, 56

Hollanders, 19 (note)

Homer, cf. also *Iliad*, 2 (note), 7, 11, 12, 18, 21, 22, 36 (note), 45 (note), 47, 65, 70 (note), 105

Horace, 26 (note), 51 (note), 52 (note), 62, 89 (note), 92 (note), 105 (note)

Iapetus, son of Titan and Terra, father of Prometheus, and fabled founder of Greece, 11

Ignorance, a nymph, nurse and attendant of Folly, 13

Iliad, cf. also Homer, 73, 105

Irishman, 30

Isocrates, Greek rhetorician and teacher (B.C. 436-338); wrote a eulogy of Busirus, which begins with a criticism of that by Polycrates on the same subject; author of many speeches and teacher of speakers, he never made public speeches because of nervousness and a weak voice, 2, 31

Italians, 30, 61

Italy, 1

Jacobines, Dominican friars, so named because the first Dominican convent in Paris stood by the Church of St. Jacques, 87

James, *St.*, *shrine of*, the shrine of St. James (the Apostle) was at Compostela in Spain, whither his body was supposed to have been transported miraculously, 70

Jerome (St.), Sophronius Eusebius Hieronymus (?340-420), Latin father of the Church, maker of the Vulgate version of the Bible, 2, 4, 82, 84, 110

Jerusalem, 70

Jews, cf. also Hebrews, 61, 82, 88

John, *the Baptist*, 160

Jove, cf. also Jupiter, 11, 12, 14, 21, 39, 40, 48, 65, 96

Julius Caesar, 115

Juno, 67

Jupiter, cf. also Jove, 12, 13, 22, 65, 67, 84

Juvenal, Decius Junius Juvenalis (c.60-c.140), Roman writer of satires in verse, famed for scurrilous exposure of vices, 4

Kolakia, or Flattery, attendant of Folly, 13, 21, 62, 73

Laelius, friend of Scipio Africanus, praised as a wise speaker by Cicero and for wisdom by Horace, *Satires*, II, i, 72, 73

Laertes, father of Ulysses; his name mentioned as a literary pseudonym, 75

Lampsacus, city at mouth of Hellespont, famed for worship of Priapus, 67

Latins, 10, 72

Lethe (river), fabled river of the underworld, from which the newly arrived spirits drink forgetfulness of their past existence, 17

Lethe, or Forgetfulness, attendant of Folly, 13, 15

Lucian, late Greek satirical writer (see introductory essay, pp. xvii-xx), wrote a mock-eulogy of a fly and a Platonic dialogue extolling parasitism; see also Pythagoras, Momus, Timon, Chiron, Micyllus, Menippus, 4, 64, 106

Lucifer, 117 (note)

Lucretius, Titus Lucretius Carus (B.C. 96-55), Roman poet whose *De Rerum Natura* opens with an invocation to Venus as creatrix of all things, 15

Lynceus, one of the Argonauts, so quick-sighted that he could see at 130 miles distance, and through rocks or trees, 39, 77, 79

Lyra (Nicholas de), mediaeval theologian (died 1340) of great learning, author of many Biblical commentaries, 110 (note)

Malea, promontory of Greece, dangerous to navigation; there is a pun on *Malea* and *alea* (dice), 55

Marcus Aurelius (Antoninus), Stoic philosopher and Roman emperor (121-180); his son, the emperor Commodus, is famed for his cruelty and outrageous vices, 32

Marpesian (stone), marble from Marpesia; the whole phrase, beginning with "as if," is from Virgil, *Aeneid*, VI, 471, describing the shade of Dido when approached by Aeneas, 39

Mars, 65, 82

Medea, wicked sorceress of Colchis; restored Jason's father, Aeson, to youth by draining his blood and pouring in a magic preparation, 19

Megarians, people of Megara, city between Athens and Corinth; in his *Adagia* Erasmus shows that the Megarians were held in low esteem, that there was "nothing to say" about them, 30

Memnon, Ethiopian king, son of Aurora and Tithonus, killed in the Trojan War, 20 (note)

Menippus, character in Lucian's *Icaromenippus* and many other dialogues; in the one named he

took a trip to the moon and viewed the world, 70

Mercury, 22, 65

Micyllus, cobbler in Lucian's dialogue, *The Dream, or the Cock*, and elsewhere in the same author; his dream was that he had exchanged places with a wealthy man and was surrounded by gold, 64

Midas, foolish king in Greek legend; awarding Pan the victory over Apollo in a musical contest, he was given ass's ears, 8, 10

Milesian virgins, at a certain period almost all the maidens of Miletus conceived a desire to die, and many of them committed suicide, 41

Milesian wool, garments of soft wool from Miletus were in great esteem at Rome, 86

Minerva, cf. also Pallas, 10, 29, 36 (note), 67

Minims, members of an austere order of mendicant friars founded by St. Francis of Paola, 87

Minors, members of one of the three orders founded by St. Francis of Assisi, 87

Minos, king and lawgiver of early Crete; after his death made chief judge in Hades, 34

Misoponia, or Laziness, attendant of Folly, 13

Momus, god of carpers; Erasmus borrows from the account of Lucian in *Hermotimus* and elsewhere, 21, 22

More, (St.) Thomas, 1-4, 64 (note)

Morychus, according to Erasmus, a nickname for Bacchus; in his *Adagia* he points out, truly, that there was a proverb, "More foolish than Morychus," but then he connects this with the smearing of images of Bacchus, arguing that "Morychus" comes from the Greek verb meaning "to befoul," 20

Moses, 61

Muses, 11, 22, 38, 51, 105

Negretos Hypnos, or Sound Sleep, attendant of Folly, 13

Neptune, 65, 67

Nero, Nero Claudius Caesar Drusus Germanicus (37-68), Roman emperor, 115

Nestor, oldest Grecian leader in the Trojan War, 18, 29, 41

Nile, 89

Niobe, wife of Amphion, king of Thebes, who was turned to stone by grief for the loss of her children, slain by Apollo and Diana, 90

Nireus, beautiful, effeminate youth in Greek legend, mentioned by Homer, *Iliad,* II, 673, 29, 60

Nominalists, mediaeval philosophical opponents of the Realists, 79

Numa, Pompilius Numa, successor to Romulus as ruler of early Rome, famed for good laws and institutions, 34

Occamists, followers of William of Occam (died c. 1349), "the invincible doctor," English scholastic philosopher, 79, 82

Odysseus, cf. also Ulysses, 47

Old Comedy, about B.C. 465-400 in Greece, consisted chiefly of political and social satire directed at persons; Aristophanes belongs to the Old Comedy, though his later work is sometimes distinguished as belonging to the Middle Comedy, 2, 20

Olympus, hill between Thessaly and Macedonia, fabled seat of Jupiter and the other gods, 15, 67

Orcus, the infernal world, personified as a god otherwise called Pluto, 11

Origen, a Greek father of the church (185-253), of great learning, 114

Orpheus, legendary Greek musician of Thrace, sometimes referred to as a poet; supposed to have been able, by playing on the lyre, to make trees move and rivers stop running; his musical power sometimes rationalized, as here, to mean eloquence, 34

Ovid, 2 (note)

Palemon, conceited grammarian (mentioned by Suetonius) who said learning would die with him, 71

Pallas, cf. also Minerva, 1, 12, 14, 20, 21, 47, 84

Pan, 8, 13, 21, 22

Paris, abductor of Helen in Trojan story, 47

Parisians, 61

Paul (St.), 63, 79 (note), 81 (note), 83, 84, 93, 99, 100 (note), 108 (note), 109, 110 (note), 113 (note), 114 (note), 115 (note), 117 (note), 117 (note), 119

Penelope, wife of Ulysses, who put off the importunities of her suitors during Ulysses' absence, by unweaving at night what she had woven in the day, 53, 82, 96 (note)

Persia, 72

Persius, a learned Roman, contemporary with the satirist Lucilius; also Aulus Persius Flaccus, a Roman satirist, but here probably the former, 73

INDEX OF PROPER NAMES

Peter (St.), 63, 79, 80, 84, 99, 100 (note)

Phaeacians, people of Corcyra (modern Corfu), famed for their luxurious living, as represented in the *Odyssey*, VI-VIII, 96

Phalaris, cruel tyrant of Agrigentum, sixth century B.C., 9, 71

Phaon, handsome young man of Lesbos, loved by many but especially by Sappho; his youth was renewed by Venus, 20, 29, 42

Pharisees, 115 (note)

Philautia, or Self-Love, attendant of Folly, 13, 29, 30, 59, 61, 73

Phoebus, cf. also Apollo, 67

Plato, favorite philosophical authority of Folly; there is a tradition that he attempted a defence of Socrates at the latter's trial but was shouted down by the body of citizens acting as judges, 23 (note), 31, 32 (note), 34, 39, 44, 49 (note), 51 (note), 64, 75, 108, 115, 119 (note), 120, 123 (note)

Platonists, 119

Plautus (Titus Maccius), Roman writer of comedies (B.C. ?254-184), 18 (note)

Plutarch, late Greek biographer and moralist (?46-?120); see Archilochus, Gryllus, the Spartan, 2

Pluto, chief god of the underworld, 65

Plutus, god of riches, father of Folly, usually represented as blind; Aristophanes' comedy of this name represents him being restored to sight, 11, 12

Poena, goddess of punishment, 65

Polycrates, Athenian rhetorician, author of a eulogy of Busirus; his name also suggested as a literary pseudonym, 2, 75

Polyphemus, the Cyclops in the *Odyssey*, IX, and elsewhere; his "lyre-twanging" is borrowed from Aristophanes, *Plutus*, 290; see also Christopher, 22, 56

Priapus, god among minor and local deities, sometimes represented as son of Venus and Bacchus, with obscene attributes; the epithet *ficulnus* (fig-wood) which Erasmus always gives him means cheap and second-rate; translated here as "ramshackle," "shoddy," and "pinchbeck," 22, 67, 91 (note), 106

Prometheus, one of the Titans, fabled to have formed men from clay and given them life and fire from heaven, 41

Pythagoras, Greek philosopher (B.C. 582-c.505); his "elemental tetrad" comes from one of the "golden verses" connected with his name: "the sacred tetrad which comprises the source and root of nature"; he taught that the numbers 1, 2, 3, and 4, or the entities represented by them added to make 10, the perfection of being; another teaching was that souls successively entered various bodies—hence Lucian's account, *The Dream, or the Cock*, of Micyllus talking with a cock which claimed to be Pythagoras himself, 15, 46

Pythagoreans, followers of above; the early Pythagoreans held goods communistically, 69

Quintilian (Marcus Fabius), Roman teacher of rhetoric (?35-?100), author of *Institutiones Oratoriae*, 32 (note), 73

Quintius Curtius, when a gap opened in the earth in the middle of the

Forum, the belief was spread abroad that only the body of a young nobleman could close it; Curtius mounted his horse and rode into it, to his death, 34

Realists, proponents, in the Middle Ages, of Realism, which taught the reality of universals, opposing the Nominalists, 79
Rhodes (island of), 67
Romans, 21, 32, 34 (note), 61
Roman See, 99
Rome, 32, 61, 70

Sagana, 91 (note)
Sappho, poetess of Lesbos (fl. B.C. ?600), 20
Saracens, 82
Saturn, father of Jupiter, Juno, and other gods, 11
Saul, 117 (note)
Scipios, the, famed Roman family; principally Scipio Africanus (major) and Scipio Aemilius Africanus (minor), destroyer of Carthage, 75
Scotists, scholastic followers of Scotus, who were Erasmus's principal aversion among his contemporaries, 79, 81, 82
Scots, 61
Scotus, Joannes Duns Scotus (?1265-1308), "the subtle doctor," Scottish scholastic theologian, 80, 82, 90, 105
Scythian, Scythia, or Tartary, was classically thought of as desert and wilderness, 30
Seius, horse of, Aulus Gellius (III, ix) tells of a clerk named Gnaeus Seius who owned a spirited horse which he sold to Dolabella, from whom it passed to Cassius and then to Mark Antony; it proved fatal or unlucky to each owner in

turn, and the proverb arose, as Erasmus quotes it, 103
Seneca (Lucius Annaeus), Roman playwright and Stoic moralist (B.C. ?4-A.D. 65), 2 (note), 39, 60 (note), 115
Sertorius, a noble Roman of c.100 B.C., 34 (note)
Seven Sages, or Seven Wise Men of Greece, a list made up of philosophers of the sixth century B.C., including Solon, Bias, Thales, etc., 25
Sibyl, Aeneas consulted the Cumaean sibyl, or prophetess, who said, among other things (Aeneid, VI, 135), et insano juvat indulgere labori, 51
Silenus, minor deity, foster-father and pedagogue of Bacchus, represented as homely, squat, and drunken; see Alcibiades, 22, 36
Sisyphus, robber of Attica, slain by Theseus, and condemned in Tartarus to keep rolling a stone up a mountain, 76
Socrates, 31, 33, 34, 51, 108
Solon, wise lawgiver of Greece, sixth century B.C., 8, 83
Sophists, in ancient Greece, popular teachers and speakers; later, in the period of the second Sophistic, similar teachers, speakers, and writers in Rome and her possessions, first to third centuries A.D., 8, 82
Sophocles, Greek writer of tragedies (B.C. ?496-406), 16 (note)
Sorbonne, college in Paris where Erasmus had encountered Scotism, 106
Spaniards, 61
Spartan, the (Lycurgus), 34 (note)
Speculum Historiale, "Mirror of History," part of the Speculum

Maius of Vincent of Beauvais (1190-1264), giving the history of the world, and containing stories used as *exempla* by mediaeval preachers, 91

Stelenus, a name suggested as a literary pseudonym; since it is not classical, Kan suggests that Erasmus meant to write Sthenelus, a name from Homer, mentioned by Horace, *Odes*, I, xv, 24, 75

Stentor, Greek in the Trojan War, famed for his great voice, 76

Stoics, "philosophers of the porch," or of the school of Zeno (B.C. 340-265); Stoic thought became influential in Rome under the Republic and early Empire; singled out by Folly as her chief opponents, the Stoics taught conformity to nature, with a rational acceptance of the universe and of human destiny, but with no exercise of hope, fear, desire, regret, or other passions; the writings of Seneca were the principal means of transmitting Stoicism to the Renaissance and modern world; Cicero and Plutarch represented a modified Stoicism, 14, 15, 22, 26, 39, 47, 51, 79

Synesius (Cyrenensis), late Greek Neo-Platonic philosopher (c. 370-430); his eulogy of baldness is extant, 2

Tantalus, a king who, for insulting the gods, was condemned in the underworld to famish for tempting fruits always out of his reach, 39

Tarentum, city of Calabria, sacred to Neptune, 67

Telemachus, son of Ulysses; his name suggested as a literary pseudonym, 75, 105

Tenedian lawyer, cf. next entry, 113

Tenedos, island and city off the coast of Troas; a "Tenedian axe" was proverbially a synonym for quick, severe justice, 78

Thales, Greek philosopher (c. B.C. 640-546), one of the Seven Sages; used as a type of wisdom, 10

Themistocles, Athenian general and statesman, 34 (note)

Theophrastus, Greek scientist and philosopher (died c. B.C. 287), who became head of the Peripatetic school founded by Aristotle; Folly's strictures upon his speaking seem to have no basis, as he was accounted a skilful speaker, 31

Thersites, in the *Iliad*, a bad-natured and repulsive railer, 2, 29

Theuth, according to Socrates in Plato's *Phaedrus*, an Egyptian god that invented numbers, geometry, and letters; Ammon, the god who ruled as king at the time, refused to accept the invention of letters on the ground that writing would impair people's memory, 43

Thomas, St. Thomas Aquinas, "the angelic doctor" (?1225-?1274), most influential scholastic philosopher and systematizer; adapted Aristotle, 84

Thomists, scholastic followers of above, 79

Thracian, 30

Thrasymachus, Athenian Sophist, interlocutor in Plato's *Republic*, whose name is suggested as a literary pseudonym, 75

Timon, Athenian of the time of the Peloponnesian War, who conceived a hatred of all people and went outside the city to live alone; subject of Lucian's *The Misanthrope*, 33

Timotheus, Athenian general, 103

Timothy, 117 (note)

Tithonus, mortal beloved by Aurora and by her made immortal; Folly neglects the circumstance, usually made much of, that he grew eternally older, though he could not die, 20 (note)

Toulouse, town in France; Aulus Gellius (III, ix) tells that when Toulouse was pillaged by Quintus Caepio and a quantity of gold was found in the temples, whoever touched a piece of the gold died a painful death, 103

Trophonius, oracle and local deity in Greece; his oracular pronouncements were given out in a cave where the ground was supposed to have swallowed him, 7

Tryphe, or Wantonness, attendant of Folly, 13

Turks, 3, 61, 82

Ulysses, cf. also Odysseus, 2, 47

Venetians, 61

Venus, cf. also Aphrodite, 15, 19, 20, 21, 51, 64, 65, 67

Virgil, see also Sibyl, Aeneas, Marpesian, 2 (note), 58 (note), 71

Vulcan, blacksmith of the gods, born lame; the "net of Vulcan" is the one he fabricated to capture Mars and Venus (Vulcan's spouse), 21, 22, 78, 84

Williamists, or Guilhelmists, friars of an order founded by William, Duke of Aquitaine, converted by St. Bernard, 87

Xenocrates, philosopher, pupil of Plato along with Aristotle; that he committed suicide does not appear from accepted accounts, 41

Youth, a nymph, mother of Folly, 12

Zeuxis, a Greek painter, fl. B.C. 430, 64

Zodiac, 89